Write for the Ear
Shoot for the Eye

Aim for the Heart

A Guide for TV Producers and Reporters

Al Tompkins

Bonus Books
Chicago and Los Angeles

06 05 04 03 02   5 4 3 2 1

Library of Congress Control Number: 2002104052
ISBN: 1-56625-176-1

Bonus Books
160 East Illinois Street
Chicago, Illinois 60611

Printed in the United States of America

Contents

DEDICATION AND ACKNOWLEDGMENTS

THIS BOOK IS DEDICATED TO:

Mrs. Patricia Miksch, Karen Jones, Janet Tandy, Doris Brown, and Patricia Yancy—my Caldwell County, Kentucky high school English, literature, and composition teachers who encouraged me to become a writer.

I owe special thanks to Polly Van Doren, news director KOLR 10-TV, Springfield, Missouri; Mike Devlin, vice president for news, KHOU 10-TV, Houston; and Les Rose, photojournalist, CBS News, for their invaluable ideas and contributions to this book.

I am indebted to my Poynter Institute colleagues Dr. Bob Steele, Gregory Favre, Jill Geisler, and Monica Moses for their ability to think critically and coach me gently.

I also thank Poynter's Library Director David Shedden for his research expertise and assistance.

My wife, Sidney, was a fountain of support and enthusiasm for this book even when I missed family outings and worked long hours writing, rewriting, researching, and staring blankly into a vacant computer screen.

I am honored to have worked with Vicki Krueger, an outstanding copy editor, and thank her for her wisdom, encouragement, and for her aggressive but judicious use of the "delete" key.

I thank the faculty and administration of The Poynter Institute, a place I respect and adore for its leadership and nurturing of journalists and journalism worldwide.

FOREWORD

THE GOAL OF THIS BOOK IS to help broadcast journalists write clearer and stronger stories. This book has three central themes.

1. **Aim for the viewer's heart.** Find, develop, and deliver stories that speak clearly to the viewer's mind while connecting with the viewer's emotions. Television teaches principally through emotions.

2. **Act ethically.** Some have the wrong-minded idea that this means "be timid in your pursuit of journalism." To the contrary, I push you to find ways to tell stories that, without solid guidelines and forethought, you might otherwise shy away from. I push you to be *more* aggressive in your coverage, not *less* aggressive.

3. **Be more interesting, more respectful, and more relevant to the viewers.** Don't pander to them and don't waste their time.

And, in some small way, I hope this book will help build and preserve the craft of journalism that has been my passion for the last twenty-five years.

INTRODUCTION

BEFORE I STARTED WRITING THIS BOOK, I asked my former publisher to tell me the most important lesson he has learned from having worked with writers for decades.

"I always tell writers not to spend too much time spitting in their hands and warming up," he said. "Get right to it. Tell me something new and interesting right away."

What great advice. Writers should get right to the story.

In my seminars, the first question I ask my participants is, "What do you stand for as a journalist?" I ask my students to write their answers down on a piece of paper. It forces them to think more deeply about the answer.

I urge you to stop reading for a moment and consider that question.

Deep down in the quiet places of your heart, what do *you* stand for? Why did you become a journalist? What dreams did you have about righting wrongs, exposing corruption, and giving voice to those who were voiceless?

In 1999, while I was teaching in Birmingham, Alabama, one veteran newscast producer began to cry when asked that question. I asked why she was crying and she said, "I no longer think of myself as a journalist. It has been so long since I thought about why I do what I do, I don't know what I stand for anymore."

If we don't know why we "do journalism," we can't hope to do it well.

After they write for a few minutes, I usually ask the participants of my seminars to share their thoughts with the entire group. The list they create usually includes these words:

What We Stand for as Journalists

Tell the truth	Hold the powerful accountable
Illuminate	Give voice to the voiceless
Inform	Be relevant
Teach	Prompt viewer action/reaction
Inspire	Alert the viewer to danger
Affect change	Educate
Be clear	Be interesting
Be unbiased	Be sensitive
Be objective	Provide context
Be honest	Be balanced

It is quite a list.

I have had the opportunity to ask groups of viewers what they think journalists should stand for. This is the list they usually create:

What We Want Journalists to Stand For

Be truthful	Be tough
Be honest	Understand our community
Be fair	Be knowledgeable/be informed
Tell us the whole story	Follow up stories
Tell us something we don't know	Find good news, not all bad
Don't exaggerate	Cover lots of topics
Don't brag	Be real and sincere
Respect privacy	Admit your mistakes

I am struck by the similarities of the lists.

So why is TV viewership declining? The single most important reason, I think, is embedded in the next two lists that I often generate with my seminar participants.

When I ask journalists "What are the most important issues facing our country and this community right now?" they say:

Most Important Issues Facing the Country

The economy	Health care/coverage
Terrorism	Environmental issues
Energy policy	Prescription drug costs
Urban sprawl/growth	Youth crime
Traffic, transportation	U.S./Foreign relations
Family values/breakdown of the family	Schools/education

Then I ask, "What stories have you given the most airtime to in the last thirty days?" The journalists make their list:

STORIES MOST OFTEN COVERED

Crime—usually drug-related murders
Accidents/Incidents (fire, flood, storms, traffic mishaps)
Celebrity news
Planned community events
Health stories, health studies, "breakthroughs"
Government scandal
Consumer tips
Politician/government official press conferences

Of course, over-arching events such as the terrorists' attack September 11, 2001 and the war that followed consumed enormous amounts of airtime for a while, but eventually we settled into the same old coverage patterns. Viewers say they are not watching because we do not thoroughly cover the stories that viewers, and even we ourselves, think are important. Somehow, television journalists have become convinced that stories that have gravity and complexity are "newspaper" stories, and not good TV.

I am convinced this disconnect is at the root of why so many TV journalists quit journalism and lose the fire in the belly that attracted them to the craft. I believe that, like that producer in Alabama, they have stopped thinking about their journalism and are focused solely on the "television" aspect of their job. Marcus Buckingham, in his book *First, Break all the Rules*, interviewed thousands of workers worldwide in a wide range of businesses. He discovered that one of the main reasons people stay in their jobs is because they "believe the job has meaning."

One of my favorite movies is *Citizen Kane*. In one scene Charles Foster Kane, a powerful and power-hungry newspaper publisher, stands in his office after putting out the first edition of his paper. He turns to his editors and says, "There is something I have got to get into this paper besides pictures and print. I have got to make the *New York Enquirer* as important to New York as the gas in that light."

Then, he writes out a Declaration of Principles to run on the newspaper's front page:

> *"I will provide the people of New York with a daily paper that will tell all the news honestly. They will get the truth in the* Enquirer, *quickly and simply and entertainingly and no*

special interests are going to be allowed to interfere with that truth. I will also provide them with a fighting tireless champion of their rights as citizens and as human beings."

In this book, I hope to give broadcast journalists the tools they need to live out that same creed. My goal is to help television journalism become more vital to the viewers and to the democracy.

Chapter 1

Aim for the Heart

"I quite agree with you," said the Duchess; "and the moral of that is—
'Be what you would seem to be'—or if you'd like it put more simply—
'Never imagine yourself not to be otherwise than what it might appear to
others that what you were or might have been was not otherwise than what
you had been would have appeared to them to be otherwise.'"

"I think I should understand that better," Alice said very politely, "if I
had it written down: but I can't quite follow it as you say it.'"

"That's nothing to what I could say if I chose," the Duchess replied, in
a pleased tone."

LEWIS CARROLL, *Alice's Adventures in Wonderland*

GREAT STORIES HANG IN THE VIEWER'S ear and catch the viewer's eye. Great stories aim straight for the viewer's heart. The best TV news stories don't just inform; they teach, illuminate, and inspire viewers.

As a reporter and later as a newscast producer, I feared that my viewers would be as confused and unable to decipher what I was saying as Alice is in the passage at the top of this page. At the end of a story, I wanted viewers to say "Ah ha!" not "Huh?"

Before I write news stories, I glance at a simple little checklist I have kept for years. The list was written by former WSMV-TV news director and later general manager Mike Kettenring. After he left a long career in television, he became a Catholic priest, so it is no surprise that the checklist is built around the word "faith."

Fair
Accurate
Interesting
Thorough
Human

Have "faith" that the power of great storytelling will connect with the viewer's heart.

The checklist keeps stories from sounding like Sgt. Joe Friday on the TV show *Dragnet*. When Sgt. Friday was on the case he would say, "Just the facts ma'am." News writing *can* be "just the facts." But the difference between *fact telling* and *storytelling* is the difference between watching the stock ticker and hearing a story about an elderly woman who has lost every dime that she needs for shelter and medicine because the market just tanked. Journalists gather facts *and* they tell stories.

But, TV reporters and producer protest, "We do TV. We write short stories. You can't be compelling *and* factual in a minute and twenty seconds."

Mark Twain, Dorothy Parker, F. Scott Fitzgerald, Edgar Allan Poe, Ernest Hemingway, and John Steinbeck learned their craft by writing short stories. They all learned what broadcast journalists know; that it is more difficult to write an interesting and contextually complete short story than it is to write a longer version of the story.[1]

With only a few words, the writer creates a hook and a complication, provides surprises, information, and character development. On television, that hook (a) captures viewers' attention, (b) brings them up to speed, and (c) leads them toward what is new in the story. Even in a twenty-second story there should be at least one main character, tension, and resolution.

Television stories and newscasts should tell tales, spin yarns, provide people with information they need to understand the world, and teach viewers something they didn't know to keep them coming back.

This chapter will help you tackle those complex stories and tell them in a way that goes straight to the viewer's heart.

In this chapter we will cover:

◇ How to find a tight story focus.

◇ How to connect the story to the viewer's heart.

◇ How television teaches through emotions more than through information.

◇ How to use soundbites to reach the viewer's heart.

---

[1] Idea adapted from Jon Franklin, *Writing for Story* (New York: Atheneum, 1986).

AIM FOR THE HEART OF THE STORY—
AIM FOR THE HEART OF THE VIEWER

Anyone who has ever written a news story, a term paper, or even a second-grade class assignment knows how hard it is to find a tight focus for the story. That skill of aiming for the heart of the story is essential to good storytelling. When she was in second grade, my daughter, MeiLin, wrote a story for class assignment called "My Luckiest Day." This ninety-nine-word tale is a clear example of what writers go through when they struggle to find a tight focus for a story. Watch what this young writer does, right in the middle of the story to correct the course of a straying narrative. (I will include the spelling and punctuation she used for added flavor.)

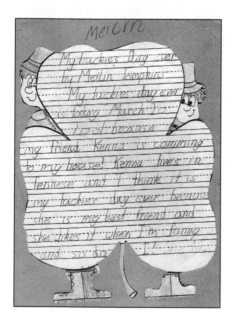 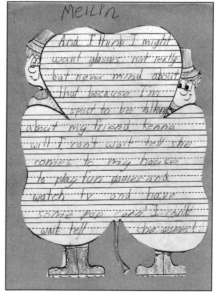

"My Luckiest Day Ever"
MeiLin Tompkins, Second Grade, Lakeview Elementary School

My luckies day ever is today March 20 2001 because my friend Kenna is coming to my house! Kenna lives in Tennese and I think it is my luckles day ever because she is my best friend and she likes it when I'm funny and so do I!

> And I think I might want glasses not really but never mind about that because I'm spost to be talking about my friend Kenna will I can't wait tell she comes to my house to play fun games and watch TV and have some pop corn. I can't wait tell she comes!

My life as a journalist would have been so much easier if, at age eight, I could have learned what my daughter learned; that great writing is a process of "selecting, not compressing" what goes in our stories. As a reporter, I have found myself in the middle of a convoluted story writing a sentence that sounded exactly like my daughter when she wrote, "never mind about that—because I'm spost to be talking about..." Journalism is an endless process of "editing out" not "leaving in" information and details.

The single most important question a writer can ask before he or she begins to type is, *"What is this story about?"* This book, for example, could have been about "writing" but that would have been a broad book about all kinds of storytelling, from folk tales to fairy tales to news writing. A book about writing might have covered how to write instructional manuals, technical documents, and scientific journals.

This book could have been about "broadcast writing," but that book might have covered everything from writing for sit-coms to documentaries. Instead, I choose to talk directly to people who write news stories. I have narrowed the focus. It is the first step in writing more powerful stories. Here is how my decision-making might look:

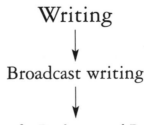

Writing
↓
Broadcast writing
↓
Writing for Producers and Reporters

Focus and get narrow. By telling narrower but deeper stories, writers help viewers understand information more clearly. This process of finding focus is really about simplifying the story. But writers know that that simplicity is deceptive. It requires skill and craftsmanship to simplify a story. In order to focus a story, the writer must understand it more fully.

Nigel Holmes, a graphic design expert, recently gave me a copy of a tiny little book he wrote. The whole book is three times the size of a matchbook. The book is called *The Smallest Ever Guide to the Internet*. It is remarkably informative and interesting. When I asked Nigel what he thought his book represents, he said, "It shows that the more you know about a subject, the more concisely you can tell the story." It seemed counterintuitive to me. And yet, that central truth about writing and storytelling holds great implications for producers.

The best way to write an effective short story is to know everything you can know about the story. Then ask yourself:

"What is the most interesting part about this story?" (This is the main thrust of the story.)

"What surprised me?" (This may be the lead.)

"What did I learn that I didn't know before?" (This is a main surprise, which we usually put high in the story.)

"What will viewers want to know? In what order will they ask those questions?" (This will determine the story frame.) If viewers urgently want to know the information, for example, the writer probably would use an inverted pyramid: "Get the urgent news at the top." If the writer is trying to explain or set the scene for a story, then a narrative style with many surprises sprinkled throughout the story might work best. In the narrative style, the viewer would wait until deeper in the piece to learn the outcome of the tale.

Ask *"What do I want the viewer to remember and feel at the end of this story?"* (This is the most memorable soundbite.)

"What comes next?" (This will lead you toward the end of the story.)

Those questions will lead you to answer this key question to help you focus your story:

"What is this story about?"

The answer should not be a long-winded account of all you know. Try to answer the question in one sentence.

Jon Franklin, a two-time Pulitzer Prize–winning writer, says writers should craft a *focus statement* about their story. He urges writers to make a commitment to what this story is about *exactly*. The "focus statement," Franklin says, "should be **three words** in length." (You can get away with a free "an," "and," or "the" without counting it.)

Let's try out this idea.

Few stories have more complexities hidden in them than stories about war. A list of the possible stories we could do about a military conflict includes:

- The generals/leaders
- The soldiers
- The civilians left at home
- The conflict involved—what is this about?
- The weapons
- The government leaders
- The foreign policies
- The history of the nations involved
- The strategy
- The diplomacy

I learned the principle of focus while watching an old Edward R. Murrow documentary film about the Korean War. CBS's *See It Now* program moved fifteen reporters and cameramen to Korea for one week to attempt to capture "The Face of the War." Here is how the program opened:

"Christmas in Korea"
December 29, 1953
     EDWARD R. MURROW: (sound of a shovel digging into frozen earth in the background) "This is Korea, where a war is going on. That's a Marine, digging a hole in the ground. They dig an awful lot of holes in the ground in Korea. This is the front. Just there, no-man's-land begins and on the ridges over there, the enemy positions can be clearly seen. In the course of the next hour we shall try to show you around Korea a bit."

It was a stunning moment for me as a young television journalist. Murrow's cameraman steadily photographed one Marine, chunking his shovel again and again against a frozen ground.

The documentary didn't include one general, not one government official. It told the complex story of the war by "putting a face on the story." The technique of "focusing the story to the little person closest to it" was one that Murrow and his producer Fred Friendly would repeat over and over on *See It Now*. Almost fifty years later, it remains the central style of the most popular news magazine programs such as *60 Minutes, 20/20, Nightline,* and NPR's *All Things Considered.*

Murrow and Friendly focused on the ordinary act of shoveling and the ordinary emotion of loneliness, which the viewer at home understood.

My three-word summary of "Christmas in Korea" is "Soldiers Endure War." The story was not about communism, it was not about foreign policy, and it was not about the generals and politicians who got us into that war. The viewer learns a lot about the war's background, but "Christmas in Korea" had a laserbeam focus on the effect the war had on the soldiers and nurses who were closest to the pain, death, and loneliness.

MURROW INTERVIEWS AIRMAN MORIARTY: "I'm Airman Third Class Brendon M. Moriarty. I was born and raised in County Kerry, Ireland. I been used to mountains all my life, but it's the mountains (of) Killarney, not the mountains of Korea. I want to wish you all a Merry Christmas. Nora, I will be home in two hundred and ninety-two days, then we will celebrate Christmas, New Year's, and St. Patrick's Day—we'll celebrate everything together. Okay darling, good-bye."

The last line chokes me up.

I remember that soundbite from Airman Moriarty twenty-five years after I first saw it while sitting in a darkened college classroom. The viewer realizes that Airman Moriarty knows, to the day, how long it will be until he is back in Nora's arms. By the time the program ends, the viewers will not remember the number of days (292) he has until he goes home. But they will always remember that *he knows* exactly how long it will be.

It is not enough for viewers to get *information* about the war. That's fact telling, not storytelling. To make the story memorable, the viewer has to *feel* something. My wife, who is a psychotherapist, tells me that **people always remember what they feel longer than what they know.**

I sometimes ask participants in my seminars and workshops whether any of them stuggled with math. Invariably hands shoot up (an interesting common trait of journalists; many of us are bad at math). I ask the participants if they remember being asked, in the fourth grade, to go to the chalkboard and work out a math problem in front of the class. Of course they do. I ask why they remember that, and the answers are touching. High-powered professional journalists confess in front of a crowd that they were embarrassed by how they felt when they got the answer wrong in front of their elementary school class.

But then I ask a key question, "What was that problem you were trying to work out?" Of course, nobody remembers. The illustration is complete; **they remember what they feel far longer than what they know**.

I believe this ability to teach through feelings is the key strength of television. Other media have other strengths. There is something about the tactile nature of newspapers that allows me to learn by cognitively interacting with the information. I can read it again and again to understand the story and information more deeply. The Internet allows me to learn by interacting with information on the screen. Radio allows me to learn by imagining. But television is unique in its ability to teach through emotions and sensory experiences.

In 1993, all the things I learned from studying Murrow's "Christmas in Korea" shaped how I approached a Christmas and war story.

Christmas Eve 1993, I was assigned to cover the pre-dawn return of soldiers from the 101st Airborne Division who were returning to Fort Campbell, Kentucky, from their tour of duty as "peacekeepers" in Somalia. I knew that in all likelihood, there would be twelve or more television cameras at the event. I guessed that most of us were walking into the story with the same focus: Soldiers come home. The question is, how could we do something different, something more memorable?

Driving to that story on that cold Christmas Eve morning, photojournalist Randy Palmer and I made a quick list of what we thought we might photograph and include in this story.

The list included:

- Families waiting
- People giving soldiers gifts
- A military band
- Tears/people crying
- The airplane
- People hugging
- Soldiers getting off the plane
- Speechmaking by officials
- Flags
- File/historic pictures from Somalia
- People cheering

We knew that every other crew covering the story had a similar checklist in mind. We asked ourselves if there were other possibilities. We considered:

- "What if we could find somebody who comes home, but nobody is there waiting for them?"
- "While everyone else focuses on the typical picture of a soldier coming home, could we find the husband of a female soldier who has been waiting for her return?"
- "Will any of the families of soldiers who died in Somalia be there?"
- "Some soldiers are still in Somalia. Will any of their families be there?"

The Army gave us no access to the waiting families until moments before the plane landed. The other TV crews scrambled to get shots of the taxiing charter transport plane. They shot wide shots of the crowded tarmac and panned the assembled crowd. We stuck by the side of a woman and her young son.

"Soldier Comes Home"
Al Tompkins and photojournalist Randy Palmer
December 24, 1993

TOMPKINS: Marla Denson has been here before on the airport tarmac...waiting. To be an Army wife, you have to get good at waiting.

MARLA: Come on, you ready to go see Daddy? (Close-up of shivering son)

TOMPKINS: Her husband, Charles, left for Somalia in August. When he left, the Army's mission in August was to feed a million starving Africans. (file tape) But the mission changed into an ugly shooting war. Marla knows that other families have waited in her same spot. Their husbands will never come home.

MARLA: It's their jobs, they have to do it, they have to do it.

TOMPKINS: How do you get good at waiting?

MARLA: Prayer, God, family, and friends; them's the four things. If you don't have them, you can't make it.

TOMPKINS: Judy Gross has gotten good at waiting. She has spent twenty years waiting for her husband, the colonel, to come home from this place or that. This is an unexpected blessing, because nobody knew they were coming home until two days ago.

(nat sd of cheering—people coming off the plane)

JUDY GROSS: Christmas when he was in Saudi, we just kept him in our thoughts and our prayers and we drank a toast to him on Christmas Eve, and that is about all you can do. You just have to think positive thoughts when they are not around.

TOMPKINS to Marla: What did you say when you heard he was coming in?

MARLA: I love you. (laughs) I have to love him. He did his job and now it is over.

TOMPKINS: One by one, the reunions happened around her. (pictures of a mother screaming then hugging her daughter) Parents screamed at the site of their children. Husbands held closely to their wives in uniform. (picture of hands) But she waited. (picture of Marla straining to see the plane) She began to think, maybe he wasn't on this plane. (pause) Maybe there was a problem.

MARLA (still looking past the camera, squinting, watching the last few soldiers come down the stairs from the plane): You have to be the mother and the father while they are gone. You have to do everything together.

(in the distance—a man shouts) Hey—Hey!

MARLA: That's you! That's you! I love you, Charles! I love you, I love you, I love you, I LOVE you, Charles, I love you, I love you, I love you.

(She kisses him repeatedly as Charles struggles to hold his hand out to his young shivering son who has waited silently.)

CHARLES (to his son as he picks him up): Hey—Hey man, come here!

TOMPKINS: Corporal Charles Denson was home, home to be with his wife and his son. She brought him a rose, because, she said, he was always bringing her roses. She worried her hair didn't look right, she asked him a thousand times if he was okay.

One hundred and fifty other Fort Campbell soldiers are still in Somalia tonight. What they wouldn't give to be where he is. He is home for Christmas.

Al Tompkins Channel 4 News, Fort Campbell, Kentucky.

┌─────────────────────┐
│   **STOP!**   │
└─────────────────────┘

Take just a few minutes before you read further to answer a question about the focus of the story you just read. In one sentence, how would you describe what this story is about? How would you describe it in three words, a noun, a verb, and an object? In other words, who did what?

When I play this story for seminars and workshops, I ask participants to tell me the focus of this story in three words.

They usually say:

- Soldier Comes Home
- Home for Christmas
- 101st Comes Home
- Families get Present
- 101st Completes Mission
- Fort Celebrates Return
- Soldiers Rescue Somalia

All of these could be good stories. They are *not* the story we produced.

I think our story was about Marla.
I think the main action Marla took was "waiting"
She was waiting for "Charles"

So the focus of the story was "Marla Awaits Husband." Or "Family Awaits Daddy."

The verb here is key. Let's see how and why we weaved the theme of "waiting" through this story

The first sentence of copy said, "Marla Denson has been here before on the airport tarmac…*waiting*. To be an Army wife, you have to get good at *waiting*."

The second section of copy included, "Marla knows that other families have *waited* in her same spot. Their husbands will never come home." Then I ask Marla the question, "How do you get good at *waiting*?"

The third section of copy said, "Judy Gross has gotten good at *waiting*. She has spent twenty years *waiting* for her husband, the colonel, to come home from this place or that."

All of that *waiting* builds the tension, so when Charles does finally come home, the viewers get a memorable emotional release.

Why did we choose waiting as a central theme? Randy and I were looking for the common experience the people standing on that tarmac had with our viewers. We know most viewers are not in the military, most are not Army wives. But everyone has waited. And remember, this was Christmas Eve, a time of *waiting*.

Waiting became the one experience that everyone who saw that story and everyone we met at that airport shared.

REMEMBER: Focus your story to one sentence, or even three words. Ask yourself, "Who did what?" Answer that question with a noun, a verb, and an object. Find a tight focus that connects with the viewer's head *and* heart. Viewers remember what they feel longer than what they know.

CHOOSING AND WRITING TO SOUNDBITES

Great stories turn on great soundbites. Let's use the "Soldier Comes Home" story to study what makes a soundbite work well.

Here are the soundbites we used:

MARLA: It's their jobs, they have to do it, they have to do it.

MARLA: Prayer, God, family, and friends; them's the four things. If you don't have them, you can't make it.

JUDY GROSS: Christmas when he was in Saudi, we just kept him in our thoughts and our prayers and we drank a toast to him on Christmas Eve, and that is about all you can do. You just have to think positive thoughts when they are not around.

TOMPKINS to Marla: What did you say when you heard he was coming in?

MARLA: I love you. (laughs) I have to love him. He did his job and now it is over.

MARLA (still looking past the camera, squinting, watching the last few soldiers come down the stairs from the plane): You have to be the mother and the father while they are gone. You have to do everything together.

(in the distance—a man shouts) Hey—Hey!

MARLA: That's you! That's you! I love you, Charles! I love you, I love you, I love you, I LOVE you, Charles, I love you, I love you, I love you.

| STOP! |

Look carefully at those soundbites. What do you notice? None of the bites contain facts. They are only opinions, emotions, and observations from the people who are closest to the story. Nobody else could have said what those people said with the same authenticity. Don't fall in love with soundbites. If the soundbite does not relate to the main meaning of the story, drop it.

Now let's look at the copy—the words I spoke as the reporter.

TOMPKINS: Marla Denson has been here before on the airport tarmac…waiting. To be an Army wife, you have to get good at waiting.

TOMPKINS: Her husband, Charles, left for Somalia in August. When he left, the Army's mission in August was to feed a million starving Africans. (file tape) But the mission changed into an ugly shooting war. Marla knows that other families have waited in her same spot. Their husbands will never come home.

TOMPKINS: Judy Gross has gotten good at waiting. She has spent twenty years waiting for her husband, the colonel, to come home from this place or that. This is an unexpected blessing, because nobody knew they were coming home until two days ago.

TOMPKINS: One by one, the reunions happened around her. (pictures of a mother screaming then hugging her daughter) Parents screamed at the site of their children. Husbands held closely to their wives in uniform. (picture of hands) But she waited. (picture of Marla straining to see the plane) She began to think, maybe he wasn't on this plane. (pause) Maybe there was a problem.

TOMPKINS: Corporal Charles Denson was home, home to be with his wife and his son. She brought him a rose, because, she said, he was always bringing her roses. She worried her hair didn't look right, she asked him a thousand times if he was okay.

One hundred and fifty other Fort Campbell soldiers are still in Somalia tonight. What they wouldn't give to be where he is. He is home for Christmas.

Al Tompkins Channel 4 News, Fort Campbell, Kentucky.

What do you notice about the copy? In this story, the *copy* includes all facts and details that explain what the viewer is seeing on the screen but would not understand if I didn't explain it.

I didn't say in the copy, "She hugged and kissed him. She was so happy to see him." The viewer could see that. I wanted viewers to know what Marla said she worried about (her hair); I wanted them to know why she brought him a rose (because he was always bringing her roses).

Fine reporters, such as ABC's Jim Wooten, use this guideline of subjective sound and objective copy to turn complex issues into razor-sharp stories.

Covering the 1988 presidential campaign, Wooten reported (September 26) on the claims that candidates George Bush and Michael Dukakis made in their first presidential debate. He lets the candidates' soundbites make claims, then his tightly focused copy sets the claim squarely against the record. As you read this passage you begin to understand why I don't buy the argument that some reporters and producers make that because of time restrictions, they can't cover issues of substance. Wooten does.

DUKAKIS: I was a leader in the Civil Rights movement in my state and in my legislature.

WOOTEN: Well, he did propose an antidiscrimination commission once, but that was about it.

BUSH: I want to be the one to banish chemical and biological weapons from the face of the Earth.

WOOTEN: But he was the man who cast three tie-breaking Senate votes for new chemical weapons.

BUSH: The governor (Dukakis) raised taxes five different times.

WOOTEN: The governor also cut taxes eight times, and people in thirty-three other states pay a greater part of their income in taxes than citizens of Massachusetts.

BUSH: I am proud to have been part of an administration that passed the first catastrophic health bill.

WOOTEN: In fact, the administration opposed some of the key provisions in that bill, and the president signed it reluctantly.

In four subjective soundbites and objective four sentences, Wooten hits solidly on four substantial issues.

Once you learn and teach others this guideline of subjective sound and objective copy, you won't have to settle for those awful and predictable interviews that producers too often see from cops or public information officers. Anyone who has conducted an interview with a stiff talking police officer knows what the typical interview includes:

REPORTER: What do we have here officer?

OFFICER JONES: We have a white male, shot twice with a large caliber weapon. The deceased died on the scene. An investigation is underway.

The only story focus that would come out of that line of questioning would be: "Shooting kills man."

It is not a new or even an interesting story.

Every producer groans when he or she hears the interview. Some news directors, in an act of frustration, have even banned interviewing "officials" in an attempt to get rid of the objective soundbite. Questions that include the word "what" usually produce responses that are factual. *"What time is it?" "What happened here?"* They are important questions, but the answers usually produce better copy than soundbites.

Producers and photojournalists must coach their reporter colleagues to ask subjective questions.

How about this:

> REPORTER: Officer Jones, you were the first person on the scene. What went through your mind when you saw this body in the middle of the street?
> OFFICER JONES: I said to myself, not again. This is the third murder this month.
> REPORTER: You have been working this side of town a long time. How safe is our town?
> OFFICER JONES: I think the city is safe, but this area right here, these ten city blocks are a real problem. We've got to get a handle on this. This is crazy.

This interview might give us the basis for a much more interesting focus: "Murder troubles officer."

The *subjective soundbite* guideline also makes it easier to pick bites from speeches and long ceremonies. Be alert for the opinion, feeling, or emotion. That is the bite that creates the lump in the viewer's throat.

REMEMBER THIS: As you aim for the viewer's heart, use *soundbites* for the subjective part of your story (*the thoughts, opinions, feelings, and emotions*); use *copy* for the *objective* part of your story (*the facts and the details*).

Chapter 2

The Shape of the Story

"A blank piece of paper is God's way of showing a writer how hard it is to be God."

JOEL SALTZMAN, *If You Can Talk, You Can Write*

IN THIS CHAPTER WE WILL COVER:

◇ The power of surprises in storytelling.

◇ When and why to use different story frames.

◇ How to write a powerful and memorable close.

STORIES NEED SURPRISES

You reach the viewer's heart by sneaking up on it. Great writers embrace the element of surprise. I learned this lesson one day when Irving Waugh walked into my newsroom. Mr. Waugh is quite simply one of the most important people in Nashville, Tennessee. He is the retired CEO of the Grand Ole Opry and Opryland. The Opry had long been associated with WSM radio and TV. Mr. Waugh cast a long shadow.

He didn't know me, but, boy, did I know him. I had seen his silver hair, athletic frame, and distinguished face in WSM-TV's archive photographs. I was the newly installed news director of that station (now WSMV) when, one morning, Irving Waugh strode into the newsroom unannounced. He walked confidently and wore a finely tailored gray suit. He was a man who thought big thoughts. His diction was perfect. He had been a radio correspondent reporting from the Philippines during World War II. His voice still had that mellow bass radio announcer tone.

My insecurities kicked in. "Was this a friendly visit or an inspection?" I was sorry I had chosen a soup-stained tie to wear that day.

I timidly introduced myself and offered him my sweaty hand, which he shook firmly.

"Lad, what's on the program tonight?" his voice boomed. He wanted to know what was going to be on this evening's news.

"Well," I stammered, "Tonight, we have a nice piece about..." He cut me off.

"Surprise me, lad," he said. "I don't get surprised much by what I see anymore." I don't recall him saying anything else as he turned on his polished heel and left.

I was hell-bent on not disappointing him, that night or ever. From that day forward, the phrase "Surprise me, lad" shaped the way I thought about my writing and my story selection. Stories need surprises. Newscasts need surprises. Mr. Waugh needed surprises.

Think about how you would tell the story to your friends or your family over dinner. You would not start with how the story turns out.

Boyd Huppert, an outstanding storyteller and reporter at KARE11-TV, Minneapolis, passes along some advice that he says helped him. "The little surprises in stories are like little gold coins that you can give to your viewer as a reward for staying with the story. Every ten seconds or so, writers should stick in one of those gold-coin moments. Just treat the story as if it were a forest trail, sprinkling the gold coins down the trail. Don't put all of the coins at the beginning of the trail; there will be no reason to keep walking. Don't make viewers walk all the way to the end of the trail; they might never get there."

It is a great metaphor for producers to use as well. Don't stick all of the gold coins in the first block of the newscast. Sprinkle the memorable gold coin stories and surprises throughout the newscast. One reason so many viewers tune out of newscasts at the end of the first quarter-hour is because they have become accustomed to producers putting all of the news in the first ten or fifteen minutes of the newscast. Viewers get wise to the fact that night after night some producers build newscasts where the important news is followed by the weather, then comes the fluff news, celebrity updates, and sports. Get some gold coin stories deeper in the newscast to reward the viewer for sticking with you.

REMEMBER: Stories need surprises. Surprises make viewers feel something. When you aim for viewers' hearts, they remember what they felt. You reward the listeners for giving you their attention.

STORY FRAMES AND FORMULAS

A big reason so few stories surprise viewers is that so many stories look the same. It's no wonder, considering how much television news reporters and producers write. Television newsrooms look like sausage mills. Everyone is churning out copy, story after story. Reporters write packages, re-cuts, Internet versions, and, if they have a convergence partner, they may also write a version to run in the newspaper. Producers write teases and stories, and some even write promotional copy and online news. TV journalists write so much in such a hurry that they may find themselves writing from formulas they have developed. The formulas swallow gold-coin moments and never give them back. Formulaic writing gives viewers the sense that they have heard the story before, even if the details are new. The story "sounds like" stories they have heard before.

Any producer could tell you the formulas they write in a crunch. How many times have I written the words:

"A funeral was held today for..."

"Police are investigating..."

"A local family is lucky to be alive."

These formulaic phrases have no meaning. They jump out of our computers because, in a crunch, writers type whatever pops into their heads. And once a phrase works, it will pop out again and again when the writer is crunched.

Memorizing formulas does not make you a writer any more than memorizing $E=MC^2$ makes you a physicist. Still, there are some formulas or, as writers sometimes call them, story frames, that endure. When producers and reporters are working on deadlines, story frames can help them write clear and easy-to-follow stories quickly.

As a reporter, when I was in a hurry and needed to write a story within minutes of an event, I fell on this news storytelling formula.

Once upon a time...	(the setting)
Suddenly...	(the complication)
Fortunately...	(the resolution)
As it turns out...	(the closing/summary)

The story is easy on the viewer's eyes and ears because the structure is so familiar to us all. You heard it when you were a little child in stories such as this one:

"Once upon a time there were three little pigs..."
"Suddenly...a Big Bad Wolf appeared and planned to eat the pigs..."
"Fortunately the third little pig made his house of bricks and the wolf could not blow it down..."
"As it turns out, they were safe in the brick house. They sang 'Who's Afraid of the Big Bad Wolf?' and danced the night away."

Even old biblical tales written about events that occurred as early as 2000 B.C. follow this story frame. One of the oldest tales in the Bible, the story of Job, follows this frame exactly.

There was once a rich and faithful man named Job. **(Once upon a time)**
Satan told God that if things turned bad for Job that Job would turn on God. God said nonsense; Job would always remain faithful. The test began. **(Tension builds)**
Job lost his animals to raiders. A ball of fire fell from the sky and killed his servants. A big wind blew and killed all his children. **(Suddenly)**
Satan covers Job head to toe with boils. Job's friends try to convince Job that he must have done something wrong for all of this stuff to happen to him. Job struggles to figure out why his sweet life has turned so sour. He wants to die. He begs God for a just hearing. He can't understand why good things happen to bad people and bad things happen to good people like him. **(Complication)**

As it turns out Job takes on God, face to face, demanding to know the meaning of all of this. God is not happy about it. God tells Job that as a man, he can't understand why all of this bad stuff happens; it just does. Job learns that he doesn't know everything; he repents.
(Fortunately)
In the end, God gives Job a new family and fortune. Job lived another 140 years and saw four more generations before his death. **(As it turns out)**

Now remember that is a four-thousand-year-old story, and it follows the same frame as many of the things you write for the six o'clock news!

But sometimes, great stories can turn the old traditional story frames on their heads. They can look like this:

As it turns out	(what happened)
Once upon a time	(the background)
Suddenly	(the main action of the story)
Fortunately	(conclusion)

Here is a story that follows the upside-down story frame. KARE11-TV's Boyd Huppert and photojournalist Gary Knox start this story in the present time. They go back in time to give context and background, then the story moves back to the present time again.

It is a story that started with a news release. Photojournalist Gary Knox (who was the 2000 National Press Photographers Association Photographer of the Year) says he was running late to work his 2 P.M. to 11 P.M. shift. When he arrived at the afternoon editorial meeting a story landed in his lap that everyone else was avoiding. It was a story that was based on a press release. Knox says the press release read something like this:

To: All News Media
Re: Press conference
Where: 1030 Morgan Street
The City of Minneapolis will announce the demolition of a building that's been a problem in a Minneapolis neighborhood.
A Press Conference will be held at the site of the building at 3 P.M.
After the Press Conference, crews will begin to demolish 1030 Morgan.

> The Mayor, the City Manager and the Police Chief will be on hand to answer media questions.

Knox and Huppert said they quickly asked to be sent out on the story. Knox said the assignment manager could not understand why one of America's best photojournalists and one of the country's most honored local reporters would ask to be assigned to cover a news conference. They clearly had a vision for the story that went far beyond a news conference.

This is the kind of story most photojournalists, reporters, and producers hate because everyone already knows how the story will turn out. The city will destroy a building. Where is the suspense and storytelling opportunity in that?

Huppert and Knox knew the main story they wanted to tell was not centered around the news conference, the mayor, the city council, or even the wrecking ball. They wanted to know why the city was making such a hoopla over the demolition of one old vacant building.

As you read this story, look for the story focus, the gold coins, and memorable moments. Look for the subjective sound and objective copy.

"1030 Morgan"
Gary Knox and Boyd Huppert, KARE11-TV

(Sound of a pile driver driving posts into the ground—pictures of a fence going up—pictures of broken windows in an old abandoned window)

BOYD: At 1030 Morgan, any sound but gunshots is good sound.

(More sound of pile driver—pictures of bullet holes in brick walls of the building.)

BOYD: But these sounds qualify as music.

NEIGHBOR: It is 1030 Morgan, the most notorious building in Minneapolis.

(pictures of man putting up "Caution Do Not Enter" tape)

BOYD: An apartment house measured not just in units but in bodies. (file pictures of a shooting victim being carried out on a stretcher)

NEIGHBOR NUMBER TWO: People getting killed, violence, and everything guns.

BOYD: In a six-month period last year, police answered 261 calls here.

NEIGHBOR NUMBER THREE: It's just a bad building.

BOYD: One of them, Denise Holland's.

DENISE: One of them grabbed me, threw me down and said, "Give me your money." I told them I didn't have no money, the other one hit me. One stomped me and one cut me on my arm. (picture of the scar on her arm)

YOUNG MAN: I seen this dude get his neck…(making a slicking motion with his hand)

NEIGHBOR NUMBER FOUR: It's a demon, that is what I call it. That building ain't worth standing there.

(sound and pictures of the bulldozer moving in)

BOYD: The demon at 1030 Morgan is about to be exorcised. (The arm of a front-end loader swipes across

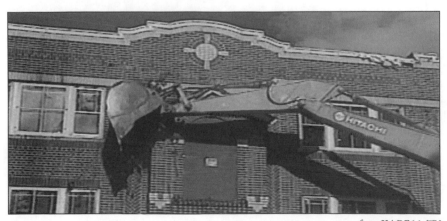

the front of the building, knocking a chunk out of the front wall; the crowd cheers.)

BOYD: Neighbors fought for years to get to this day. (woman uncorks a bottle of cheap champagne)

(bystanders clink champagne glasses) "To 1030 Morgan—1030 Morgan."

BOYD: But it was the moment they savored.

NEIGHBOR NUMBER FOUR: I don't sit out here in no sun for nobody, I am going to sit and watch this building get tore down.

(The tractor's arm goes up for another swipe at the building—more bricks fall.)

BOYD: Yet out of the dust, the mist, and the sun came a symbol.

(The water from a firefighter's hose being used to settle dust helps to create a rainbow.)

NEIGHBOR NUMBER FIVE: Do you see the rainbow? Yea.

BOYD: A sign of hope.

DENISE: I think when that sucker comes down, people will start healing.

BOYD: Ten years of violence has ended (pictures of a black girl and a white boy standing side by side watching) with one last act of destruction.

from KARE11-TV

(Man walking with a hunk of bricks he picked up.) This is for all the ones that passed away. I am going to take it home with me.

BOYD: The death of 1030 Morgan.

NEIGHBOR NUMBER TWO: Hallelujah.

MAN WITH BRICKS: For all the ones who ain't here. (He walks away with his arms full of bricks.)

Boyd Huppert, KARE-11 News, Minneapolis.

The typical frame for this story might have been: *City destroys house.*

But Gary and Boyd framed a more personal and intimate story. They framed the story about the demolition at 1030 Morgan as: *Neighbors celebrate demolition.*

The story focuses *less on the building* at 1030 Morgan St. and *more on the people* who had been affected by the drug dealing and crime that had set up residence there. Because they include the feelings and emotions of the people most closely affected by the demolition, the story becomes memorable and relevant, even to those of us who do not live near the neighborhood.

Hourglasses and Pyramids

We live in a time when viewers want to know the news quickly. Between a third and a half of all viewers watch TV news with the channel changer in their hands or within quick reach. Producers and writers know this. That's why they rely on the inverted-pyramid style of "news first, details later." It's a reliable delivery system in breaking or spot-news reporting, because getting the outcome of the story "up high" is vitally important to the viewer.

This time-honored news frame has been successfully used in stories for more than a century.

Former CNN assignment editor and now journalism professor/historian David T. Z. Mindich says that the inverted pyramid style may have been first used in reporting of President Abraham Lincoln's death.[1]

There are many examples from that night. The Associated Press reported, Friday, April 14, 1865: *"The President was shot in a theater tonight and perhaps mortally wounded."*

---

[1]David T. Z. Mindich, *Just the Facts: How "Objectivity" Came to Define American Journalism* (New York: New York University Press, 1998), 65–67.

The writer, Lawrence Gobright, packed the most important news right in the opening sentence. Gobright filed a second dispatch that took readers on a chronology of the evening, but the opening sentence gave the reader a reason to want to know why the reporter was writing about Lincoln's visit to Ford's Theatre.

The New York Herald and *The New York Times* reported the story the next morning. Both newspapers led their coverage not with stories written by reporters, but with memos written by Secretary of War Edwin Stanton. Professor Mindich says Secretary Stanton's account of Lincoln's dying hours "may very well be one of the first inverted pyramids in history." The event in journalism history has its own brand of irony since Stanton had a reputation of being a press censor during the Civil War.

On April 16, the *Herald* published Stanton's dispatch:

> This evening at about 9:30 P.M. at Ford's Theatre, the President, while sitting in his private box with Mrs. Lincoln, Mrs. Harris and Major Rathburn, was shot by an assassin, who suddenly entered the box and approached behind the President.
>
> The assassin then leaped upon the stage, brandishing a large dagger or knife and made his escape in the rear of the theatre.

The report was a little less direct than the stark AP version, but the main information still showed up in the first sentence.

The New York Times' lead story was also pyramid shaped but without the hard summary lead sentence.

> War Department, Washington
> April 15—4:10 A.M.
>
> To Major-Gen. Dix:
> The President continues insensible and is sinking.
> Secretary Seward remains without change.
> Frederick Seward's skull is fractured in two places, besides a severe cut upon the head.
> The attendant is still alive, but hopeless. Maj. Seward's wound is not dangerous.
> It is now ascertained with reasonable certainty that two assassins were engaged in this horrible crime, Wilkes

Booth being the one that shot the President, and the other companion of his whose name is not known, but whose description is so clear that he can hardly escape. It appears from a letter found in Booth's trunk that the murder was planned before the 4th of March, but fell through then because the accomplice backed out until "Richmond could be heard from." Booth and his accomplice were at the livery stable at six o'clock last evening, and there left with their horses about ten o'clock, or shortly before that hour.

It would seem that they had for several days been seeking their chance, but for some unknown reason it was not carried into effect until last night.

One of them has evidently made his way to Baltimore— the other has not yet been traced.

Edwin M. Stanton
Secretary of War

My favorite reporting from that night came from *The Star Extra*, which used the inverted-pyramid style along with some microscopic detail. *The Star Extra* reported:

At 7:20 o'clock the President breathed his last, closing his eyes as if falling to sleep, and his countenance assuming an expression of perfect serenity. There were no indications of pain and it was not known that he was dead until the gradually decreasing respiration ceased altogether.

Rev. Dr. Gurley, of the New-York Avenue Presbyterian Church, immediately on it being ascertained that life was extinct, knelt at the bedside and offered an impressive prayer, which was responded to by all present.

Dr. Gurley then proceeded to the front parlor, where Mrs. Lincoln, Capt. Robert Lincoln, John Hay, the Private Secretary, and others, were waiting, where he again offered a prayer for the consolation of the family.

The following minutes, taken by Dr. Abbott, show the condition of the late President throughout the night.

11 o'clock—Pulse 44.

11:05 o'clock—Pulse 45, and growing weaker.

11:10 o'clock—Pulse 45.

11:15 o'clock—Pulse 42.
11:20 o'clock—Pulse 45; respiration 27 to 29.
11:26 o'clock—Pulse 42.
11:32 o'clock—Pulse 48 and full.
11:40 o'clock—Pulse 45.
11:45 o'clock—Pulse 45; respiration 22.
12 o'clock—Pulse 48; respiration 22.
12:16 o'clock—Pulse 48; respiration 21; echmot. both
             eyes.
12:30 o'clock—Pulse 45.
12:32 o'clock—Pulse 60.
12:35 o'clock—-Pulse 66.
12:40 o'clock—Pulse 69; right eye much swollen and
             echmoses.
12:45 o'clock—Pulse 70.
12:55 o'clock—Pulse 80; struggling motion of arms.
1 o'clock—Pulse 86; respiration 30.
1:30 o'clock—Pulse 95; appearing easier.
1:45 o'clock—Pulse 86; very quiet, respiration irregular.
             Mrs. Lincoln present.
2:10 o'clock—Mrs. Lincoln retired with Robert Lincoln
             to adjoining rooms.
2:30 o'clock—President very quiet; pulse 54; respiration 28.
2:52 o'clock—Pulse 48; respiration 30.
3 o'clock—Visited again by Mrs. Lincoln.
3:25 o'clock—Respiration 24 and regular.
3:35 o'clock—Prayer by Rev. Dr. Gurley.
4 o'clock—Respiration 26 and regular.
4:15 o'clock—Pulse 60; respiration 25.
5:50 o'clock—Respiration 28; regular; sleeping.
6 o'clock—Pulse failing; respiration 28.
6:30 o'clock—Still failing and labored breathing.
7 o'clock—Symptoms of immediate dissolution.
7:22 o'clock—Death.

The tiny details in the story, including the exact pulse rate gives the reader vital information about how doctors hoped the president might pull through. An hour later, we can see that Lincoln's condition grew more grave. Just after dawn, he died.

The New York Times includes another strong example of pyramid-style storytelling from that day.

> Andrew Johnson was sworn into office as President of the United States by Chief Justice Chase, to-day, at eleven o'clock. Secretary McCullough and Attorney General Speed, and others were present.
>
> He remarked: "The duties are mine. I will perform them, trusting in God."

After the death of President Lincoln, Professor Mindich says, "the character of newswriting changed." Newspaper reporters (and, later, TV and radio reporters) had discovered a formula for putting the most important news first. But the structure lacks the "gold coins" that pull a viewer through a story all the way to the end.

To build up to a pivotal moment in storytelling, writers have another shape at their fingertips: the hourglass. In the hourglass, the top of the story holds the important news, but with a twist. It is followed by a transition to keep viewers' interest, and supported by details of the event. The hourglass can hold the viewer's heart from top to bottom.

Let's look at a story by KARE11-TV reporter Phil Johnston to see how these story frames play out in day-to-day reporting. Johnston and photojournalist Brett Akagi came across a car on fire. It was a fairly typical story except for one big detail—which they planted about a third of the way into the story.

This is a strong example of a daily news story that goes well beyond the inverted-pyramid style into an hourglass shape.

"What I've Got Is What I've Got"
Phil Johnston/Brett Akagi, KARE11-TV

(Sound of siren—pictures of flames—water spraying on the fire.)

PAUL HAWKINS: (talking to firefighter) I pulled off the freeway and I saw smoke coming and I said, "Maybe just the pipe got hot."

REPORTER: Almost as soon as Paul Hawkins's '89 Celebrity caught fire, on Hamlin Avenue near I-94, the St. Paul fire department had it out. But you would be amazed how quickly your world can change...

from KARE11-TV

PAUL: I stay in Minneapolis, but I live in my car.

REPORTER: ...when you are homeless.

PAUL: Everything I own, my whole life, pictures of my mom, my family, my ID, everything I basically own.

REPORTER: Since moving from Kentucky to Minnesota this winter, Paul Hawkins has made a home of his car while looking for work. For all practical purposes, for no apparent reason, his home was destroyed today.

PAUL: (With a disgusted look, he tosses burned belongings into the car.) Well, what I got is what I got. I lost my gloves, my hats, every damn thing.

REPORTER: And when you consider that Paul Hawkins' everything wasn't much to begin with...

PAUL: My whole damn world.

REPORTER: It kind of makes you wonder, why?

PAUL: (As he walks away from the burned-out shell of his car) You know, you take a forty-year-old male, ain't nobody gonna help me. I'm fixing to be on my own again.

REPORTER: In St. Paul, Phil Johnston, KARE-11 News.

Let's rewrite the story in a typical inverted-pyramid style.

REPORTER: A car fire destroyed everything that forty-year-old Paul Hawkins owned today. Hawkins, who has been out of work, lived in his car. The 1989 Chevy Celebrity caught fire this morning while he was driving on Hamlin Avenue near I-94 in St. Paul. Nobody was hurt. But firemen couldn't save Hawkins' belongings from the flames. He lost his hat, gloves, even pictures of his mother. Now he is left with nothing.

PAUL: (With a disgusted look, he tosses burned belongings into the car) Well, what I got is what I got.

REPORTER: Hawkins is not sure what he is going to do next. With no home and all of his belongings destroyed, he wondered how he can start over.

PAUL: You know, you take a forty-year-old male, ain't nobody gonna help me. I'm fixing to be on my own again.

REPORTER: Firemen are not sure how the blaze started.

PAUL HAWKINS: (Talking to firefighter) I pulled off the freeway and I saw smoke coming and I said, "Maybe just the pipe got hot."

REPORTER: In St. Paul, Joe Smith, Channel 99 News.

In the first story the shape looked like this:

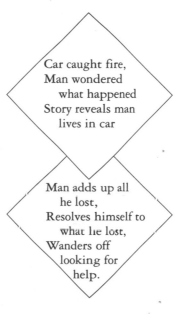

Car caught fire,
Man wondered
what happened
Story reveals man
lives in car

Man adds up all
he lost,
Resolves himself to
what he lost,
Wanders off
looking for
help.

If they had used an inverted pyramid frame, the story might have looked like this. This version has no gold-coin surprises. It is all fact and no heart.

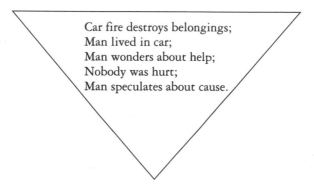

Car fire destroys belongings;
Man lived in car;
Man wonders about help;
Nobody was hurt;
Man speculates about cause.

Which story do you think a viewer will remember? Look at the focus, the three-word summary, and see how the soundbites help a viewer feel, as well as hear, the story. When the writer makes the viewer feel the story, the writer has *aimed at the viewer's heart*.

REMEMBER: There are many kinds of story frames. Inverted pyramids get the important news in the first sentence. It is especially useful for covering breaking news that answers the question of "what happened?" Hourglass frames allow the writer to sprinkle surprises throughout the story. The hourglass frame is most useful when the story's goal is to answer questions of context such as "How often?", "Why?", "What else should I know?"

"WELL, TIMMY"

NBC News/*Today Show* correspondent Bob Dotson says that most great stories have what he calls a "Well, Timmy" paragraph near the end of the story.

"If you ever watch the old show *Lassie*," Dotson explains, "then you will know what I am talking about. See, somewhere late in every episode, Dad sits down with little Timmy and sorts the story all out for him. 'Well, Timmy,' Dad might say, 'You see the little birds have to learn to fly away from their mother, and even if we want to help them, they have to learn to be on their own, without our interference. Someday you will want to fly away from Mom and me, do you understand son?'" Dad wisely resists the temptation to tidy up the fact that sometimes nature takes it's painful course. Journalists should also resist the temptation to tidy up an untidy story. The good guy does not always win; sometimes stories do not resolve themselves.

THE BIG CLOSE

Don't spend all of your energy on the first half of your story only to allow the piece to run out of gas. Save one last morsel for an "ear-catching close." It's the big finish. The close to the big sale. The grand finale of the fireworks display. What you say and show at the end of the story is often what lingers in the viewer's heart.

The closing often works best if it connects with the opening in some way closing the circle. The last sentence usually should be short and tight. It should contain only one main thought that summarizes the whole story. The last sentence must directly connect to the three-word focus statement you write for your story.

As I think about the pictures that I will write to, I usually go for what an old photojournalist friend, Don Cadorette, called the "negative action shot."

At the end of the story, Don liked to have the subject walking away from the camera. If he used a zoom, he zoomed *out* at the close, not *in*. He wanted the viewer to physically detach from the story, as you would if you walked away at the end of a conversation. It is less jarring than close-up, or with someone walking toward you.

The best closing to a story is like a good ending to a meaningful phone call. In order to write a great close, be sure you know how you want the viewer to feel at the end of the story. Aim at the viewer's heart. You will get there through the viewer's eyes and ears.

REMEMBER: Just before the story closes, the story-teller should, in one sentence, summarize the main point of the tale. Then, deliver the big close that comes back to the main conflict you established at the beginning of the story.

Chapter 3

Find Memorable Characters

"What lies behind us and what lies before us are tiny matters compared to what lies within us."

RALPH WALDO EMERSON

RON TINDIGLIA WAS A LITTLE MAN who became a news industry giant. "Giant" was his favorite descriptor of anything that was big, exciting, or important. Ron, at age twenty-nine, rose from producer to news director of WABC (New York), later was general manager at WCBS (New York), and became vice president of news for the CBS television stations (CBS O&O). Later, he became a consultant/confidant/mentor/coach for countless news executives, including me.

After I became news director at WSMV-TV, Ron gave me a note that I posted on my bulletin board. It read:

"Put a face on every story. Our stories are about the people we serve. We should serve people with our stories."

That little sign and that little man taught me that great stories need great characters. Characters are usually people, but they can be objects such as an old church, an overgrown cemetery, a pristine lake, or a dying swan. Each of these images evokes an emotion in the viewer. Characters are the mechanism we use to deliver information and tell the story. After all, people remember what they feel longer than what they know. A story about a tornado is more interesting if you can tell me about a child whose toy was blown away, along with his house. Storms are interesting, but not as interesting as children. Aim for the viewer's heart by putting a face on the story.

In the chapter we will cover:

◇ How to use a memorable character to tell the story.

◇ How to tell big stories through small examples.

Put a Face on the Story

Kim Riemland, a masterful storyteller who reported for KOMO-TV, Seattle, mined the richness of characters in her stories. One day, Kim says, the station asked her to "run by the courthouse and grab something" about a routine sentencing hearing in a murder case. "The desk" thought the story might be only thirty or forty seconds on the newscast. When she got to the courthouse and listened to what are sometimes dry courtroom routines, however, she found a remarkable story. In fact, she plays off the "routineness" of this proceeding in her opening line. Then she "puts a face" on the routine hearing to make the story powerful and memorable.

"Sentencing Day"
Kim Riemland, KOMO-TV, Seattle
August 8, 1997

(Deputy leads handcuffed prisoner into courtroom.)

KIM: It is case number 96-dash-C-dash-07-dash-90-dash-9. That is how the courts see it. But to the woman in the second row, this is the day the man who killed her husband will be sentenced.

ALYCE LOUCKS: David and I were partners in life. Not just another married couple, (accused criminal hangs his head and leans on table in front of him while woman speaks) not just best friends, but inseparable souls, seeking our future together, our hearts were forever entwined.

KIM: Alyce and David fell in love as kids, at Seattle University. As adults, they married. She was David's wife. Now, Alice Loucks tells the judge what it is like to be his widow.

ALYCE: As surely as David suffered a torturous, cruel, physical death at the hands of Joseph Gardener and Shawn Swenson, so, too, have I suffered a torturous and cruel emotional death. The difference is David is now free from his pain, and I must live with mine every day for the rest of my life.

KIM: David owned this North Seattle recording studio. It was here that he was living his dream. And it was here that he died. One night in March of 1995, two men tied David up, they beat him, strangled him, they put duct tape over his nose and mouth. They stole equipment from his studio,

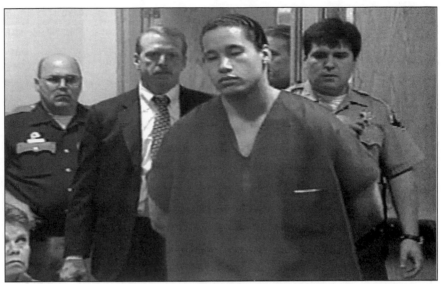

from KARE11-TV

and they stole David from all the people in this courtroom. Alyce has thought about what David would say to the man who killed him.

ALYCE: I wanted to make music, and live and love and laugh. And I would have helped you make music, too, you fool. You didn't have to hurt me. Hell, I would have helped you carry those things out to your car, if you would have just let me keep my life.

KIM: Those who loved David asked that Joseph Gardner get an exceptional sentence. But when he spoke to the judge, he did not ask for leniency.

GARDNER: I did that and I never tried to sit there and fool myself or anybody else about it. I am willing to accept whatever the court is willing to give.

KIM: The judge made her decision and, two and a half years after David's murder, case number 96-dash-C-dash-07-dash-90-dash-9 is over. Joseph Gardner will spend almost therty years in prison. Alyce Loucks will spend the rest of her life without her husband.

At the King County courthouse, Kim Riemland, KOMO News 4.

Kim chose the theme "Wife mourns loss." The story focuses almost exclusively on Alyce Loucks.

The *Seattle Post-Intelligencer* covered the same hearing. Reporter Paul Shukovsky chose a different theme. He used minute details to paint the picture of the courtroom for the reader. For Shukovsky, the main character in the story was not one person, but a collection of people who shared one emotion—sadness.

"Studio Owner's Killer Gets 29-year Sentence"
Paul Shukovsky, *Seattle Post-Intelligencer*
August 9, 1997 *(used with permission)*

A 24-year-old man who pleaded guilty to the 1995 strangulation of a North Seattle recording studio owner was sentenced yesterday to almost 29 years in prison.

Joseph A. Gardner acknowledged that his role in the slaying of David G. Loucks, 34, was committed in the course of stealing his audio equipment.

Gardner's accomplice, Shawn Swenson, was found guilty of first-degree murder Tuesday.

On March 7, 1995, Swenson distracted Loucks by pretending to record a rap song at the studio, 4033 Aurora Ave. N. Meanwhile, Gardner slipped up behind Loucks and placed him in a chokehold, according to prosecutor Kerry Keefe.

Loucks was zapped by a stun gun, bound and gagged with duct tape and beaten while he was hogtied face down. Loucks' father, Allan Loucks, found his body the next day.

As family and friends sobbed softly, the elder Loucks yesterday told how discovering the body left an indelible mark of terror on him. And he beseeched King County Superior Court Judge Patricia Aitken to send Gardner to prison for life.

"I go to bed at night thinking of my poor son lying on the floor and being beaten by these animals."

The victim's wife, Alyce, told Aitken: "Two lives were lost that night. For just as he was tortured and murdered…so, too have I…suffered a torturous and cruel emotional death. The difference is David is free from his pain, and I must live with mine for the rest of my life."

Gardner, dressed in a red jail jumpsuit, stood before the bench with his head bowed, occasionally glancing toward Alyce Loucks.

Gardner reached for a tissue, wiped his nose, then told Aitken, "I did that. I am willing to accept whatever the court is willing to give."

After Gardner's arrest, he cooperated fully with police and prosecutors and testified against Swenson during his trial.

Because of his cooperation, Keefe asked that Gardner be sentenced to 25 years.

But instead Aitken sentenced him to 347 months, saying that if not for his cooperation, she would have given him an even harsher sentence in excess of state sentencing guidelines.

Swenson will be sentenced Sept. 5.

The newspaper story focus might be summed up in three words as "Court sentences killer," or "Sentencing ends ordeal." Because the newspaper story was less focused on Alyce and focused more on the proceeding, Paul included microscopic details about what went on in the courtroom.

"Gardner, dressed in a *red jail jumpsuit,* stood before the bench with *his head bowed..."*

And:

"Gardner *reached for a tissue, wiped his nose..."*

Even though the stories are very different in tone and focus, the reporters chose two of the same quotes/soundbites:

"Two lives were lost that night. For just as he was tortured and murdered...so, too have I...suffered a torturous and cruel emotional death. The difference is David is free from his pain, and I must live with mine for the rest of my life."

And:

"I did that. I am willing to accept whatever the court is willing to give."

Both writers knew the power of a subjective soundbite. The quotes were thoughts, opinions, feelings, and emotions that only could have come from the person closest to the story. Those soundbites allow the viewer to get into the skin of the character, to share that person's pain, sense of loss, frustration, and loneliness.

LITTLE PICTURES, BIG STORIES

Edward R. Murrow's "Christmas in Korea" documentary for *See It Now* fouses on the names, faces, fears, and hopes of soldiers stuck in the crossfire of war. The show ends with a platoon making plans to walk directly into harm's way. It is the ordinariness of the orders that make the plans seem all the more chilling.

> SERGEANT: I am gonna assign a recon patrol tonight, men, and these will be your jobs. Chambers, you will be number one scout. Ball will be number two, second man in the file. I'll be third scout. Wallace, you carry the AR, the basic load of ammunition. Archebeck, you follow Waley. Smith, you come after Archebeck, and Kim, follow Smith. Smothers behind Kim, and Lee carries the radio. Sisson, you pack the wire, and Sergeant Lammar, you are second in command. You will be in the rear. All right, let's move on.

One soundbite, a dozen young faces. Murrow's "put a face on it" style reminds viewers that people fight wars, not machines, not governments. It is a war about *people*, ordinary people with names such as Waley, Smith, and Chambers.

By putting a face on the story you use the little picture to demonstrate the big picture. That skill is at the core of how Murrow took on Sen. Joseph McCarthy. Murrow's long-time producer Fred Friendly said, "We had always been under pressure to do something about McCarthyism, and he kept saying to people who came to see us about it, 'Look we're not preachers; we cover the news. When there is a good news story about McCarthy that will give us a little picture, we will do it. But we are not going to go make a speech about McCarthy.'"

That little picture came in the form of a newspaper clipping Murrow handed Friendly one day. "The story in the *Detroit News* said, 'Radulovich fired,' and Ed said, 'This may be our McCarthy story.'"

The CBS *See It Now* team began looking into the case of Lieutenant Milo Radulovich, who had been tossed out of the U.S. Air Force Reserve in 1953 because his sister and father read a Serbian language newspaper from time to time. Milo's father had immigrated to the United States twenty-six years earlier and liked the newspaper's Christmas calendars, he said. The Air Force considered Milo to be a communist sympathizer because his sister and father read a newspaper that some considered to be "communist leaning." The program went right for the heart. It said, right up front, that nobody in the Air Force ever had a problem with Milo's loyalty or performance.

Here is the opening to the story:

MURROW: This is the town of Dexter, Michigan, population, 1,500. This statue is at the head of Ann Arbor Street. "Erected by the citizens of Dexter to the heroes who fought and martyrs who died that the Republic might live." This is the story of Milo Radulovich—no special hero, no martyr. He came to Dexter one year ago, after ten years in the Air Force, won a general commendation for working on a secret weather station in Greenland. Now he is a senior at the University of Michigan eight miles away. His wife works nights at the telephone company. They live at 7867 Ann Arbor Street. This is Milo Radulovich.

Murrow stripped the bark off the Air Force. He showed the government's case was built almost completely on unnamed sources whom Milo could not confront. Radulovich was not allowed to see the sealed documents the government said it had gathered that proved his guilt. *See It Now* interviewed townspeople, other so-called "little people," about what was happening to Milo. Murrow's crew interviewed John Palmer, the town's chief marshal, and Madeleine Lewis, who worked at the dry cleaning store down the street from where Milo lived. CBS interviewed the town dentist and the gas station owner. To learn more about Milo's father, CBS interviewed the recording secretary for the United Auto Workers, of which Milo's father had been a member for two and a half decades.

The interviews were a masterful stroke. Each person interviewed had nothing to gain by sticking up for Milo, and they had so much to lose. They easily could have been branded as communist sympathizers for being critical of the government. But the theme of their comments cut to the heart of the story: "If this could happen to Lieutenant Milo Radulovich, it could happen to any American, and the people behind it should be stopped."

The program generated so much mail, so much heat, that five weeks after *See It Now* took on Milo Radulovich's case, the secretary of the Air Force, Harold Talbott, reversed the government's decision with the simple statement, "He is not, in my opinion a security risk." Milo had his life back.

"He (Murrow) believed this was a nation of little people, and he befriended them in real life and on television," Fred Friendly said years later. "He loved little people who stood up against the crowd, and I think that is the essence of what Ed, who had a modest beginning and had to fight for a place in the sun, believed in."

This is a timeless technique. Jesus, in the New Testament, spoke in simple stories about everyday people. He told short stories, such as the one about the widow who gave all she had to the temple. He told the parable of a man and his prodigal son. He "put a face on every lesson." He used simple examples to teach complex concepts.

The Chinese philosopher and teacher Confucius (whose real name was Kong Qiu) frequently taught his students in simple sentences, thoughts, and stories. Often those stories were about the actions or obligations of one man, not all mankind. For example, "He who is not concerned about what is far off will soon find something worse nearby." And "To see what is right and not do it is cowardice."

Great storytelling clarifies complexity. When journalists cover the local planning and zoning meeting, they don't just tell the viewer what the council decides; they tell us how the decision will affect the community, and who it will affect the most. As Murrow did, look for the little guy who is fighting city hall. Look for who will profit most and how they influenced the process.

When covering the tornado that rips through a county, focus less on the damaged barns and trees, and focus more on the people who didn't have insurance and now have to find a way to rebuild. When you cover a flood, remember the high water is not interesting unless it affects someone. Who is fighting the rising water by building sandbag dikes? Who stayed up all night evacuating his home? The water is the *what* in the story, but the people are the *who*. Viewers will not remember how many feet the river rose; they will only remember it rose enough to harm the old woman whose house got washed away.

Great writing helps viewers understand how nuclear power plants work, why countries fight, how viruses spread, and why rivers flood. Edward R. Murrow said television journalism can "educate, illuminate, and inspire." That happens more often when storytellers tell the big story through strong but small characters.

REMEMBER: Put a face on every story. Tell complex stories through strong characters. The best characters are those who are closest to story/issue.

Chapter 4

Write Inviting Leads

"There are three simple rules for turning out a near-perfect piece of writing. Unfortunately, no one knows what they are."

SOMERSET MAUGHAM

SWEAT THE LEAD. THE FIRST sentence of your story sets the main conflict in motion. It reflects the focus. The lead deserves the energy you pour into it. The lead is a compass that points to the heart of the story.

Writers always toil over leads. Songwriters know that the lead is everything. In music and in news, the lead can set up the main conflict. Read the first sentences in some of my favorite songs:

"You never close your eyes anymore when I kiss your lips."

Righteous Brothers

"She was just 17, and you know what I mean."

The Beatles

"Something's happening here. What it is ain't exactly clear."

Buffalo Springfield

"Yesterday, all my troubles seemed so far away..."

The Beatles

"Why don't you love me like you used to do?"

Hank Williams

"It won't be easy, you'll think it strange when I try to explain how I feel, that I still need your love after all that I've done."

From *Evita*

"Hit the road, Jack, and don't you come back no more, no more, no more, no more..."

Ray Charles

In just a phrase or two, leads can set up tension and set a scene. Here is the dynamic open to "Something's Coming" from *West Side Story*:

> *Could be!*
> *Who knows?*
> *There's something due any day,*
> *I will know it right away,*
> *Soon as it shows.*
> *It may be cannonballing down from the sky,*
> *Gleam in its eye,*
> *Bright as a rose!*

Before you write, study your notes or the wire copy from which you are writing. Then, before you begin writing, put your notes away. The story you are about to write is in your head, not in your notebook. Check your notes for accuracy, but you will find that the details you have forgotten to include are probably best left out.

My young children and I like to watch *The Flintstones*. When Fred Flintstone tries to run, he jumps up in the air, his feet go round and round, underscored by the sound of a bongo drum. Then—zoom—he takes off like a shot.

Avoid writing what I call "Fred Flintstone leads." Don't allow your leads to run in place. Get right to the reason that viewers should spend some of their valuable time with you. If reporters would adopt this idea, they would immediately improve their live reporting.

"Get some news in the first sentence," my Poynter colleague and a former news director Jill Geisler told her reporters at WITI-TV, Milwaukee. "Don't stand in the convention hall and tell me you are live at the Joe Blow for Governor campaign headquarters. Tell me where he is, what he is doing, tell me what he will do next. Give me some news in the first sentence."

In this chapter we'll cover:

◇ Crafting a lead that hooks viewers.

◇ Eliminating clichés in leads.

FIRST IMPRESSIONS

About every other month, my father drove my brothers and me "into town" where we would sit on the worn wooden benches of Charlie's Barber Shop and wait our turn to get a buzz cut. There wasn't much happening outside the barbershop window in Fredonia, Kentucky to distract a young boy from a long wait. The barbershop sat between Talley's Grocery and Cox's Feed Mill. For as long as I can remember, barber Charlie Phelps had a sign tacked to his wall featuring a demure woman who wore pearls and a sensual black dress. In the picture, she was looking over her shoulder as if she was leaving a cocktail party with somebody very lucky. Under her face, a caption said, "You never get a second chance to make a first impression. It pays to be well groomed."

All of those hours I spent fantasizing about that woman in the poster served me well when I became a journalist. Her lesson about good grooming applies to TV news writing. Your first sentence creates the viewer's first impression of the story. The lead should not overwhelm; it need not be the peak action of the story. But it should cast a wide net that captures as many viewers as possible. Your opening sentence should be as inviting as the smile of that woman in the picture.

Say you are doing a story about river pollution. You could open with cold statistics about how much toxic smoke belches each day from a nearby chemical plant. But consider starting with some copy about a bear that depends on this stream for his daily meals of salmon. I care about the bear. So I might stick around to hear how the factory's emissions hurt the bear or, worse, hurt people living nearby. I believe viewers see a story lead as the invitation to stay or the temptation to leave.

Veteran broadcast journalist and Syracuse University associate professor Dow Smith says, "The most effective lead refers to some aspect of the story that is important or interesting to the audience—the hook."[1]

Smith says a lead about a tax increase, for example, should not start by saying, "The city council voted to raise property taxes by ten cents per one hundred dollars of assessed land value." The lead should tell the viewer what the vote means: "The city council is raising your taxes $600." Smith says, "The best lead lines involve the audience by relating the news to them."

Great leads answer the viewers' question: "So what? Why is this a story I should watch?"

The story lead should not tell me how the story will turn out. The story lead is not the story. The lead is the gateway to the story. It is the

---

[1] Dow Smith, *Power Producer,* (Washington, D.C.: Radio-Television News Directors Association, 2000), 43.

lure. It is the journalists' best pitch for why a viewer should invest a little more time with that station.

I sometimes challenge journalists who attend my workshops to write the story of Little Red Riding Hood as a news story. Invariably, they write the lead:

"A Woodlawn Lane girl narrowly escaped being eaten by a wolf today."

It gets right to the point, but there is not much left for the storyteller to say once the viewers know that the girl got away from the wolf safely.

In almost two centuries since the story of Little Red Riding Hood was first published, writers have changed many details of the tale. In versions written in the middle 1800s, the writers called her "Little Red Cap." In some versions the little girl takes a jug of wine to her grandmother. In others she is carrying a pot of warm butter. By the early 1900s, the storytellers say her basket contains little cheesecakes. In some versions, the wolf eats the little girl. In other versions, the wolf eats the grandmother but not the little girl. Some of the old versions became controversial because the wolf invites the little girl into the grandmother's bed, and librarians warned parents that the story had sexual overtones.

While researching this book, I have read more than twenty versions of *Little Red Riding Hood*. In every single version written over more than 200 years, *not one* gives away the outcome in the lead. They all build suspense by telling the reader how lovely the little girl is and how sweet she is to care for her sickly grandmother.

The writers have known all along that the story has to make the reader "feel" something for the little girl before they care whether the wolf eats her.[2]

So, if we were writing this tale for the newscast, we might write the lead:

> **Tonight, we bring you the tale of a little girl who tried to help her sick grandmother. But the young girl ran into a problem. A big bad problem. Channel 9 reporter Carl Grimm picks up the story.**

That story lead would appeal to young and old. It gets right to the conflict. It creates some suspense and starts the "big and bad theme." The lead does NOT give away the outcome.

---

[2]To read sixteen versions of Little Red Riding Hood written from 1729–1916, go to "The Little Red Riding Hood Project," edited by Michael N. Saldan for the de Grummond Children's Literature Research Collection, University of Southern Mississippi. The entire project is available online at *http://www-dept.usm.edu/~engdept/lrrh/lrrhhome.htm.*

A note of caution: When you write story leads, don't play games with the viewer. *Saturday Night Live* included a skit in which the TV anchor announcer says, "The president is dead, but president of what? We'll have that story coming up."

Of course, that's just silly. Don't bury critically important information just to build suspense.

SOME DOS AND DON'TS FOR LEADS

- **Attribution before action**

   First, tell viewers who is talking, so we will know whether we believe the source.

   Not: *"It was a case of arson, that, according to police..."*

   Better: "Police say an arsonist set the fire."

- **No More Fred Flintstone leads**

   Not: *"First up tonight, our lead story tonight, topping the news tonight, the big story tonight, in the news tonight, as we have been telling you, as we told you, we start tonight with the latest on this still developing story."*

   Just get on with it. Author and writing teacher Merv Block asks, "Why do writers tell viewers they have been telling us a story for days? If the viewer does not know that, then telling us you told us does not help us."

- **"Home" is where the viewer is**

   Not: *"Here at home," "closer to home."* Drop those "running in place" phrases. I once worked at a station that covered four states. "Here at home," to our anchors, meant here in Paducah, Kentucky, where our studios were. But "here at home" could have meant here in Missouri, or Illinois, or Tennessee to our viewers who lived in those states.

- **Do not continue to use the word "continues"**

   Not: *"The jury continues to deliberate tonight."* News is what's new. If something continues, it is not new; it is just a continuation of what is old. Use the lead to tell viewers what is new. Think how you would tell me the "newest news" if you came home to dinner and tried to tell me what you did at work today. "The people standing outside the county courthouse are asking each other why the jury has been out so long." "The D.A. is wondering whether he should have taken this case to trial." Find something new and get it in the lead.

- Avoid "if you"

  Not: *"If you have children, watch this story."* This means if I don't have children, I can turn away. "If you like Jell-O…" What if I hate Jell-O? Can I watch *Baywatch* instead and not worry that I missed something important on the news? Don't give viewers a chance to change the channel. The only "if you" lead I can think of that might hold viewers is, "If you have a pulse, you should watch this story." That would cover pretty much everyone who we are trying to serve.

- Seldom start with a number

  Not: *"Forty-nine-year-old Joan Johnson is angry that the county wants to raise her taxes."* You have given me a reason to care about her. Her age should not be in the story unless it matters to the story. If officials are raising her taxes *because* she is forty-nine, then the age stays in the story, just not in the lead. Let's turn the sentence around. "The county wants to raise her taxes and Joan Johnson is angry."

  Think back to *Little Red Riding Hood*. How old was Red Riding Hood? It doesn't matter. She was little. That's all I need to know.

  Scott Libin, the grammar-loving news director at KSTP-TV in Minneapolis, asks reporters, "Would you say, 'I'm going over to see my grandmother tonight. The seventy-eight-year-old widow is not feeling well.'?" Libin says he is convinced reporters include ages and dates in their leads because it makes copy look more complete, and it makes reporters and producers think they are including important details in their stories. Libin says, "When age matters, use it."

  "If a ten-year-old robs a bank, then the age belongs in the lead. If a thirty-year-old robs a bank, their age is probably not newsworthy."

- Give information before identification

  Not: *"Joe Smith is a killer, police say."* Tell the viewer who is making the accusation first; so we would write "Police say Joe Smith is a killer."

  Not: *"Reginald M. Demarcus is in jail tonight, charged with burglary."* Viewers associate details about the person with the person's name, but they need the details first. Think how much easier it is to remember somebody's name at a cocktail party when she says, "Hi, I'm Joey's cousin, Sylvia," rather than, "I'm Sylvia, Joey's cousin." You can almost hear yourself saying, "Oh, Joey's cousin, now what's your name again?"

Not: *"In Las Vegas, the rain is coming down."* If I missed the city name, I missed the whole story. Maybe something like, "You don't expect floods in the desert, but Las Vegas flooded today."

- **Kill the clichés**

    Not: "Candidates for governor *hit the campaign trail* today." It's not nice to hit.

    Not: "It was *every mother's worst nightmare.*" What exactly is a mother's worst nightmare?

    Not: *"apprehended."* Can we just say " arrested" or "caught"?

    Not: "Investigators are *sifting through the rubble* tonight looking for clues." Really? Are they sifting? My grandmother sifted flour. I have covered a lot of fires, I have never seen firefighters sift through rubble. (Except for the months after the attack on the World Trade Center in New York.)

    Not: "Eighteen people are *confirmed dead.*" If they are not confirmed, let's not call them dead.

    Not: "Negotiators *held talks* today." Why not say they "met"?

    When we report on car wrecks, why do writers feel a need to say somebody *"suffered contusions and abrasions"*? Could we just simplify it to "cuts, bumps, and bruises"?

    Not: "Negotiators sat down at the *bargaining table* today." The company and the union started negotiating; they talked or met. There is no special table around which negotiators meet called a "bargaining table."

    Not: "Police are on high-alert tonight, this *in the wake of...*" Wake is for water and funerals: Just say "after."

    Not: "Police suspect *foul play* in the death of a young girl.*" Murder is not play; it is serious. Police say somebody killed the young girl.

    Not: "Police are looking for an *armed suspect* tonight." A suspect is *a specific person* police have in mind. If cops do not know for whom they are looking, then journalists should label the person by their criminal type, such as a robber, burglar, or rapist.

    Not: *"deceased."* Let's be honest, the guy is "dead." Same for *slain* and *fatalities.* Somebody or some thing killed them.

    Why say *"incarcerated"* when you could say "in jail"?

Why do writers call them *"hot water heaters?"* If the appliance in your garage heats water, shouldn't we call it a water heater?

Other phrases that could "suffer a tragic death": *the right stuff, out stumping, ground zero, a real horse race, warts and all, bandwagon, bargaining chip, pins and needles, rank and file, some say, officials say, reportedly, tempers flared, hot and heavy, changes hands, close call, a new lease on life, innocent bystander, innocent victim, firestorm, lone gunman, disturbing, surprising, shocking, fantastic, stunning, denies allegations, confirms allegations,* the *Bible Belt, lucky to be alive, amazing, breathtaking, sigh of relief, it's a miracle, major breakthrough, medical miracle, Iraqi* (or insert other country) *strongman, time will tell, too soon to tell, last but not least,* and, my favorite—*totally destroyed.*

The craft of writing demands precision. Mark Twain said, "The difference between the 'right word,' and the 'almost right word' is the difference between lightning and lightning bug."

REMEMBER: You never get a second chance to make a first impression. Leads tell me, "So what?" Leads invite the viewer to watch (or leave). The story must fulfill the lead's promise.

Chapter 5

Verbs and Adjectives

"I once used the word OBSOLETE in a headline, only to discover that 43 per cent of housewives had no idea what it meant. In another headline, I used the word INEFFABLE, only to discover that I didn't know what it meant myself."

DAVID OGILVY, *Confessions of an Advertising Man*

ONE EVENING, MY WIFE AND I watched an evening newscast. The big story was a forest fire that had burned thousands of acres and seemed destined to grow larger. The story opened with dramatic pictures of the flames. Helicopters swooped as the correspondent said:

"Smoke rising, firefighters tiring, water running out."

I looked at my wife and said:

"Verbs missing, story unclear, set off."

Television journalists are disguising verbs as gerunds. You can spot the phony verbs because they usually have an "ing" behind them. It has become such a common practice that I have actually called friends of mine at networks and asked whether they have been ordered not to use verbs. None admits to it.

Think about how silly you would sound if you came over to my house for dinner, walked through the front door, turned your nose to the air, and pronounced, "Pot roast cooking, smelling good, hungering for dinner." How did all of this start? What happened to verbs? God only knowing.

In this chapter, I will argue that journalists use too many adjectives and not enough active verbs. I will try to convince you that my concerns are more about journalism than style.

In this chapter:

◇ I will explain the difference between active and passive verbs.

◇ I will give you tips on how to write in the active voice.

51

◇   I will explain the difference between subjective and objective adjectives. You will learn why journalists should avoid subjective adjectives.

The Thing About "ing"

Every few years, television reporters and producers adopt some new way of writing that they think "juices up" copy and makes it sound more urgent. Most often, the trendy writing sacrifices active verbs for false present verbs.

They write:

"President Bush, in Washington tonight, considering what to do about Social Security."

The past, the present, and the future seem to meld together. If one watches the evening news, it might appear that all news is live; none of the information is past tense. However, almost all news, by definition, is past tense. The president might be considering what to do about Social Security right now, but he also might be taking a nap, eating dinner, or taking a bath.

Look at this example from CNN's *Moneyline* with Lou Dobbs, October 30, 2001:

"Top government officials today adding their voices to the call for Americans to remain vigilant."

Here is a story I saw on the *NBC Nightly News* May 31, 2001. Notice how the journalist only uses seven complete sentences, but all of the people she interviews speak in complete sentences. I put her complete sentences in boldface type.

KELLY O'DONNELL: Today the farewell. **In West Palm Beach, Florida, those who loved those Barry Grunow, those who learned from him in the classroom, come together to remember.**

STUDENT: It was really sad; he was a great guy. I really miss him a lot.

KELLY O'DONNELL: A teacher for nearly thirteen years, a husband to Pamela for nine, a father to five-year-old Sam, nine-month-old daughter LeeAnn.

FRIEND: He has a huge heart and he loved to work with kids.

KELLY O'DONNELL: At thirty-five, Grunow killed by a bullet fired just minutes before the school year ended Friday. The accused shooter, thirteen-year-old Nathaniel Brazill, a boy in whom Mr. Grunow actually saw promise, just recently recommending Brazill be named a peer mediator next year, helping other students resolve conflicts.

But on Friday the honor student was sent home for horsing around with water balloons. Police say he returned with this twenty-five-caliber handgun. Today, school officials mystified, the student showed no signs of trouble, no history of behavior problems.

NAT HARRINGTON (West Palm Beach schools): We still don't have any of the answers that people will ultimately get to in terms of why.

KELLY O'DONNELL (standup): One area under examination, the boy's home life, reports of domestic violence between his mother and her now ex-husband and later a boyfriend. **Police say officers were called to the home seventeen times in the last six years, but no one was ever arrested or charged.**

Tonight the school fence filled with tributes to Grunow, an English teacher who left an affluent suburban district five years ago to teach here in Lake Worth, a working class neighborhood where friends say he felt he could do more good.

PARENT, RICHARD RATHELL: You know, he was a guy of integrity. He loved his family; he cared enough about his community to come back to his community to teach.

KELLY O'DONNELL: **For his family, the loss renews old wounds. Grunow's dad died on this same day eighteen years ago. Now his two children will know the same pain.** Kelly O'Donnell, NBC News, Lakeland, Florida

Kelly O'Donnell says she intentionally writes in the "verbless" style. "If a story is complicated, sometimes a writer has to use more words and a more traditional style. But other times I want to convey emotion and experience. I want to shift some attention from what I am saying. It is like poetry where words are collected together to create feelings and ideas. Those stories are different from how prose is written. I want viewers to hear things and fill in some of the gaps so long as it is clear and understandable," she said.[1]

But there is a danger in allowing viewers to fill in the gaps. Viewers get distracted. Viewers don't watch TV news the same way journalists watch TV news. At home, viewers might watch news while they prepare a meal. They might only be half-listening to the news with a screaming child in the background. Every morning I read the paper with the TV on in the background. I contend that the passive verb style with gaps, as Kelly calls them, makes the story more difficult to understand.

She makes the case that the kind of "watching" TV that I do makes her style more useful, not less useful.

"People are bombarded by images," O'Donnell says. "When they are under time constraints I say the fewer words the better, so long as it is understandable. This style gives people an opportunity, a way of giving equal weight to consider the script, the sound, and the pictures."

But the passive style creates other problems. By not saying, in the copy, who sent the boy home, we do not know the possible motivation the boy had for shooting Mr. Grunow. The story says; "But on Friday, the honor student *was* sent home for horsing around..."

The viewer asks, "*Who* sent him home?" The passive verb "*was*" keeps the sentence from telling us the vital information of "who did what?"

"To Be" or Not "To Be"

Whether or not journalists use verbs is not just an issue of style. Writing that does not include active verbs runs counter to many things that journalists say they stand for. Let's see if we can get this straight. Any verb that is a derivation of the verb phrase "to be" is passive. My grammar teacher in high school called them "state of being" verbs. If

---

[1]Kelly O'Donnell interviewed by the author, December, 2001

something is in a "state of being," it means it is not taking action. State of being verbs include "am, is, are, was, were, be, being, been." The words "is" and "are" speak in a present tense voice, the rest are past tense. So if we say, "President Bush is considering..." then we must know for sure it is something he is doing right now.

Writing coach Valerie Hyman, who runs a company called BetterNews *(www.betternews.com),* advises broadcast writers to put themselves on a "to be" diet.

She does not tell reporters and producers to never use "to be" verbs, but tells them to "just ask if there is a more active way to write the sentence."

When I was teaching producers at a Michigan TV station I saw some copy that a producer wrote for the evening news. The story said:

"The suspicious device was found in a school bathroom."

I asked the producer, "Who found the bomb?"

"Oh," he said, "a third-grader did."

So the new sentence said:

"A third-grader found the suspicious device in a school bathroom."

Active verbs tell the viewer "who did what." Precision writers use active verbs. I find that when producers use passive voice, they usually do so because they don't know "who did what."

Let's go back to Kim Riemland's "Sentencing Day" story in Chapter Three and see how active verbs give power to stories. I underlined the active verbs.

> David <u>owned</u> this North Seattle recording studio. It was here that he was living his dream. And it was here that he <u>died</u>. One night in March of 1995, two men <u>tied</u> David up, they <u>beat</u> him, <u>strangled</u> him, they <u>put</u> duct tape over his nose and mouth. They <u>stole</u> equipment from his studio, and they <u>stole</u> David from all the people in this courtroom. Alyce has thought about what David would say to the man who <u>killed</u> him.

In that passage, we can find nine active verbs in six sentences. The active verbs give life to an event that happened months earlier.

Remember: Go on a "search and destroy mission" for verbs that end in "ing." Put your stories on a "to be" diet. Ask "Who did what?" to help yourself avoid passive verbs. The difference between active and passive verbs is the difference between "the gun was found" and "the boy found the gun."

Avoid "Fantastic, Unbelievable, Gut-wrenching" Subjective Adjectives

We each see the world through our own lens. The lens is colored by many factors such as where we grew up, how much education we have, our race, gender, ethnicity, and, for those of us with brothers and sisters, where we fall in our sibling order. We all have our own biases and experiences.

All of those experiences and points of view show themselves in our writing, especially when we use subjective adjectives. Go on a search and destroy mission to edit them out of your news copy.

I differentiate between "subjective" and "objective" adjectives because there is nothing wrong with using adjectives that are provably true and add valuable information.

An example of *subjective* adjectives might be this sentence:

"It was an *awful* scene. The *terrifying* woman slammed her husband with a *huge* frying pan."

It is the writer's opinion that the scene was "awful," that the woman was "terrifying," and that the pan was "huge."

If I used *objective* adjectives I might write;

"The *three elementary school-age* children said they were frightened when their mother whacked their *drunken* dad's head with a *seven-pound cast iron* frying pan."

The facts prove that the children were of elementary school age, that the man was drunk, and that the pan weighed seven pounds and was made of cast iron. We might pluck those facts from a police report. They add rich detail to the story. Good writers use specific details in their stories not just to convey information but to convey emotion (and viewers will remember what they feel longer than what they know).

When writers lean on worn-out adjective clichés to describe a scene, the viewer gets the sense this is not a unique or singularly important story. It is a generic tale. When we tell viewers, "Here is a story you have to see to believe," we plant a seed of doubt in the viewer's mind: "There may be a good reason not to believe it."

Recently I heard a newscaster describe a shooting as a "tragic murder," as if some murders are not tragic. Nobody needed to call the space shuttle Challenger explosion "tragic"; we all knew it was.

Other adjective clichés include *fantastic, unbelievable,* and *mother's worst nightmare.* These words show up most often in the second or third day of coverage following an event. It is as though journalists feel a need to pump air into a dying story. So we use these inflated words. The viewer knows these words are hyperbole. Worse, the words reveal the journalists' biases.

There is a famous story from Portland, Oregon's KATU-TV. The story is so unusual there are five Web sites devoted to it.

On November 12, 1970, reporter (now anchor) Paul Linnman was a witness to a whale of a problem.

An eight-ton, forty-five-foot sperm whale washed up on the central Oregon coast, south of Florence. Linnman said it had been dead for quite some time and was starting to get a bit foul. The state highway workers called on the Department of the Navy for some advice. The workers soon made a plan. Since they couldn't bury the whale (the ocean tides would soon uncover it), and cutting it up and burning it was out of the question (nobody wanted that job), they settled on simply using some dynamite. They planned to blow up the whale into pieces small enough for the crabs and seagulls to take care of.

They didn't know how much of the explosives to use. Nobody had ever done anything like this before. They took an educated guess and packed a half-ton of dynamite around the carcass, backed up onlookers a quarter of a mile away, and counted down to the explosion.

Not only did the blast pulverize only a portion of the whale, but the wind blew particles of smelly, rotten, whale flesh in the direction of the spectators, which came down on them like a spring rain.

There were large chunks spewed all over the beach including a three-foot by five-foot hunk that landed a direct hit on the roof of a brand-new Buick parked a quarter-mile away.

Thankfully, nobody was injured, except maybe the pride of the Oregon State Highway Division. In the end, workers buried the larger remains of the whale in the sand.

As Linnman said, "The Oregon State Highway Division learned a valuable, but messy lesson not so much about what to do, but as what NOT to do if they ever faced a situation like this again."

On rare occasions, I play Linnman's story for reporters and producers at seminars. I ask the crowds to think of words that describe the video of the exploding whale. They often use words like "unbelievable" and "amazing." Once in a while somebody will say "disgusting" or "sick." A couple of years ago, while doing a seminar in Oregon, I played the story and one producer said she thought what those cleanup workers did was "disrespectful." I asked why she felt that way, and she said she always felt close to whales and hated to see anything bad happen to them.

I grew up in Kentucky. I thought the exploding whale video was at least amusing, if not outright funny. The only whales I ever saw were in books or in movies.

That producer taught me a lot that day. She taught me that the descriptions we use in our stories directly reflect who we are. The main lesson we should take from the "exploding whale" story is that if we claim to write with precision in our news stories, we should limit the adjectives we use.

REMEMBER: Limit your use of subjective adjectives. They are a reflection of your own opinions and biases.

Chapter 6

The Art of the Interview

"The most basic of all human needs is the need to understand and be understood. The best way to understand people is to listen to them."

RALPH NICHOLS, *Are You Listening?*

My wife, Sidney, is a psychotherapist and sometimes she conducts relationship workshops for couples. The one-day workshop is designed to jumpstart relationships that lose their juice or slide off track. Sidney puts the couples through one exercise about listening; an exercise I have adopted (she says "stole") for use in my journalism seminars. She asks the partners to think about something critically important that they want to tell their spouse. She asks them to imagine in some detail how they will say what they have to say and how excited they will be to say it. She assigns one of the partners to act as the speaker and one is the listener. Then, she tells the listener to send clear signals that he/she could not care less what their partner has to say. Then, she shouts, "Go." Instantly, the person whose job it is not to listen begins looking away, reading a magazine; some even get out of their chairs and walk off. My wife tells me that in fifteen years of doing those workshops, she has never had one single person ask, "How do I show someone that I am not interested?" We all are experts at that. We have spent a lifetime perfecting the fine art of tuning others out. But learning to listen, *that* is a skill that is so rare that when we find somebody who really listens, we open up and tell things to that person we might never tell another soul. Great journalists learn to listen.

In this chapter, we'll explore:

◇ How to ask questions that allow the other person to talk more and allow you to deeply listen to their answers.

◇ How to focus your questions to get more focused answers.

◇ Strategies for handling difficult interviews.

◇ Guidelines for tough ethical issues that come up while inter-
    viewing sources.

◇ Interviewing "don'ts."

◇ The need for natural sound and silence in stories.

◇ Tips for using microphones effectively.

LEARNING TO LISTEN

From the moment babies are born, people start coaxing them to talk.
Adults celebrate a child's first words. Then what happens? As soon as
kids start talking, adults insist they be quiet. How odd!

The same thing happens in journalism schools. They spend so much
time training students to report and write that they miss the most
important part of reporting...listening. Listening is at the core of journalism. Every journalism school should have a formal course in how to
listen to other people.

How many times in an interview do you find yourself:

• Thinking that the subject is uninteresting
• Criticizing the speaker and/or delivery
• Listening only for facts or soundbites (bottom line)
• Taking no notes
• Faking attention
• Tolerating or even creating distractions during the interview
• Tuning out difficult material rather than trying to understand it
• Letting emotional words block the message
• Wasting the time difference between speed of speech and
  speed of thought, not processing what is being said during the
  pauses
• Interrupting the interviewee when the conversation slows
• Making statements rather than asking questions in the
  interview[1]

---

[1]Adapted from R. G. Nichols and L. A. Stevens, *Are You Listening?* (New York: McGraw-
Hill,1957), *www.listen.org*.

I teach a workshop on how to be a better listener. I usually ask journalists to write down the name of a person they know whom they would consider a great listener. Then I ask them to write down a few characteristics that show others how this person is a good listener.

The list often includes:

- They do not interrupt me.
- They make time for me, no matter what they are doing.
- They focus on me; they don't keep typing on the computer or reading the newspaper while I talk.
- They don't try to give me the answer; they don't tell me what to do. They just listen and help me think through the situation for myself.
- They ask questions to let me know they are really listening and that they are focused on my story.
- They don't judge. They just want to help.

So many of these listening skills are central to great news interviews. So how do you become a more skilled interviewer?

ASK BETTER QUESTIONS

Before you head out for any interview, do some prep work. Here are some tips to help focus your thinking.

- **Think about the purpose of this interview.** If your goal is just to gather facts, then use objective questions. If you are trying to elicit soundbites or opinions, then subjective questions are your best tool. Subjective questions usually begin with phrases such as "Why...?", "Tell me more about...?", or "Would you explain...?". Objective questions get information that will end up in your voice-over copy: "How much money did they get away with?", "Did the victim die?", "How many protestors did you count?"

- **Ask open-ended questions.** Open-ended questions cannot be answered with a "yes" or a "no." Open-ended questions do not offer a choice, such as "Do you feel X or Y?" Great conversation *starters* include "How did...?", "What if...?", "Why do...?". Questions that *stop* conversations include "Do you deny...?", "Will you...?".

- **"Mirror."** Tell your interviewee what you hear him or her saying and then ask, "Did I get that right? Is there more?" Remember not to interrupt or disagree; that blocks your ability to listen. Mirroring checks your understanding.

  • **Listen more than you talk.** Listening is more than just waiting for your turn to talk. You are interviewing in order to learn. If you are talking, you are not learning anything. Use your ears more than your mouth.

Journalists must learn what those in the healing arts have known for centuries; that much of our job is to listen. Here is a quote I found in a magazine for nurse midwives about the importance of listening. I am struck by how much journalists can learn from it.

"Listening is noting what, when, and how something is being said. Listening is distinguishing what is not being said from what is silence. Listening is not acting like you're in a hurry, even if you are. Listening is eye contact, a hand placed gently upon an arm. Sometimes, listening is taking careful notes in the person's own words. Listening involves suspension of judgment. It is neither analyzing nor racking your brain for labels, diagnoses, or remedies before the person is done relating her symptoms. Listening, like labor assisting, creates a safe space where whatever needs to happen or be said can come."[2]

The Poynter Institute's senior faculty for writing, Chip Scanlan, analyzed an October 22, 2001 Department of Defense news conference to learn what kinds of questions work best. He noticed that long-winded questions produced the weakest answers. One reporter asked a 105-word question that drew an 81-word response from Defense Secretary Donald Rumsfeld. In the question, the reporter even gave permission to the interviewee not to answer. Here was the question and answer:

> Q: Mr. Secretary, two questions…one for you and one for General Myers, if I may. You came down a couple of weeks ago and you were rather incensed about classified information—leaks of classified information, and you sort of threw down the gauntlet in this building, saying that people would be sought out and punished. Are you now trying to find out who leaked the information as to Friday's raids?
>
> And to General Myers: Even though you're not going to tell us specifically, you did give us a pretty good rundown on the Friday raids. Are commando-type raids ongoing, as we speak, in Afghanistan?

---

[2] Alison Para Bastien, "The Healing Art of Listening," *Midwifery Today E-News* (Vol. 1, Issue 50, Dec. 10, 1999).

A. RUMSFELD: As a matter of fact, I am too busy, then, to run around trying to find who did that. I don't know if anyone is, to be perfectly honest. I'd certainly hope that the people who were parachuting in don't find the person.

MYERS: In terms of ongoing—perhaps ongoing ground action, we simply can't talk about that right now. Like we said Saturday: Some things are going to be visible, some invisible. And I'm not going to get into the details.

A better way to ask those long and complex questions might have been:

Mr. Secretary, what are you doing to find out who leaked that information and; General Myers, what can you tell us about commando raids going on right now in Afghanistan?

That would be two questions in thirty words. Both questions would be open-ended, not closed-ended, so both would require the respondent to answer with more than a "yes" or a "no."

Besides the convoluted questions, the reporter seems to want the world to know he sits in on a lot of Defense Department briefings. Resist the impulse to make any statements in your questions and never editorialize ("You were rather incensed about classified information") or anticipate the response ("Even though you're not going to tell us specifically"). Let the subject do the work.

One reporter asked a terrific question that was specific, tough, and would elicit a subjective response:

Q: Well, which information reported on Friday prior to the operation do you think crossed the line?

Here is another example of a double-barrel question with an editorial twist:

Q: Mr. Secretary, what is the rationale for not explaining where the operation forces attacked the airfield over the weekend? Inasmuch as the bad guys know what was attacked and there's no big surprise to them, why not

> reveal to the American people where this operation took
> place?
>   RUMSFELD: We probably could.

Think about it. Would you say "bad guys" on the air in describing the targets of a military attack? The forty-seven-word question could have been shorter, more open-ended, and less editorial. For example:

"Why won't you say where special operation forces attacked over the weekend?" (twelve words).

• **Focus on one issue at a time.** Ask one question at a time. If you ask two questions, the interviewee will choose the question that is easiest to answer and avoid the more difficult one. One of Canada's premier investigative journalists and author John Sawatsky says, if you offer a double-barrel question, you may not know which part of the question the interviewee is answering. For example, a reporter asked Bill Clinton: "Was Gennifer Flowers your lover for twelve years?" He answers: "That allegation is false." Which allegation is false? That they were lovers, or that the relationship lasted twelve years? Diffuse questions lead to vague answers. Start by asking "Was Jennifer Flowers your lover?" Follow up with the open-ended question, "How long did the relationship last?"

The order of your questions matter. Don't lead off with: "Well, why *did* you embezzle all that money?" Ask more innocuous questions to get the subject talking before you go for the hard stuff.[3]

• **Be naïve.** A great question is, "Nah, really?" when someone tells you something surprising. It leads the person to tell you more. NBC correspondent Bob Dotson calls this technique the "non-question question." Dotson says, "When you ask your subject a question, they are going to give you the answer they think you want to hear. Then, they stare at you without you saying a word. Then, they give you the deeper, more heartfelt answer. In other words, people hate silence; let them fill it in."

Edward R. Murrow liked to share his interviewing secrets with his younger colleagues. He told new correspondents, "If you put a direct question, the interviewee will answer it as he has probably answered the same question dozens of times before. Then begins the waiting game. He thinks he has given you the definitive answer. You manage a slightly

---

[3]Susan Paterno, "The Question Man," *American Journalism Review* (October 2000): 55.

uncomprehending, puzzled expression, and you can watch his mind work. 'You stupid oaf, if you didn't comprehend that, I'll put it in language you can understand,' and proceeds to do so. Then, in the course of editing, you throw out the first answer and use the second one."[4]

Dotson tells reporters and photojournalists to spend a few minutes getting to know the people they are going to interview before they turn the camera on. But Dotson says, "Don't talk to them about the subject you really want to know about at first." Once you start the conversation, try the non-question question, "Now that looks like a fine mobile home you used to live in." People are more likely to tell you what they lost and why the home was important to them.

If you are standing near a grieving relative, just saying something such as "It's a sad day" might open the conversation by letting the person know you are empathetic. Keep in mind: Less is more. The more information *journalists* put into questions, the more information *interviewees* leave out. Short questions produce succinct, dramatic, focused responses. Long, rambling questions get long, rambling answers or curt, confused replies.

Sawatsky says, "People, by nature, are either 'inputters' or 'outputters.'" TV journalists, for instance, tend to leave their dial on output. Inputters are straight men, allowing sources to crack wise and showcase personality. "I can go into any newsroom and usually tell you who gets the best stories in the paper. It's usually the reporters with the blander personality. They're not the life of the party. They're amazingly consistent if you eavesdrop on them during interviews: You'll hear plain, neutral, bland questions. Colorless questions usually provide colorful answers."

"The best questions are like clean windows. When we ask a question, we want to get a window into the source. When you put values into your questions, it's like putting dirt on the window. It obscures the view of the lake beyond. People shouldn't notice the question in an interview, just like they shouldn't notice the windows. They should be looking at the lake."[5]

• **Be tough. Be human. Be honest.** You don't do an interview subject any favors by not asking tough questions. Ask the questions the

---

[4]Joseph E. Persico, *Edward R. Murrow: An American Original* (New York: McGraw-Hill Publishing, 1988), 419.

[5]Susan Paterno, "The Question Man," *American Journalism Review* (October 2000): 56.

public wants to know the answers to or the story will lose credibility with the audience.

However, Sawatsky urges reporters to "Ask tough questions; don't just ask tough-sounding questions." Asking a subject "Are you a racist?" is an easy question that sounds tough. The answer most certainly will be no. Instead, ask focused, open-ended questions about evidence that suggests the source is a racist."

Sawatsky says, "Put the burden of proof on the source. If a source insists, 'There was no crime,' ask, 'How do you know that?' If a source says, 'I can't remember,' ask, 'Why can't you remember?'"[6]

To focus questions, Sawatsky says, "Pick a key phrase the source mentioned and repeat it in an open-ended question. If, in describing his marriage, Ted Kennedy says, 'We've had difficult times,' respond: 'What do you mean by difficult times?'"

If you are going to really hammer a person in a confrontational interview, it is dishonest to lead the interviewee to believe this is going to be a softball conversation. While setting up the meeting, I would say, "Look, I have some tough questions to ask, but I think it would be unfair to write a story without asking you to speak to these questions." That is the sort of forewarning that you would like to be able to tell a jury if you had to defend yourself in a defamation lawsuit. It is also honest and fair and shows the subject that you want to hear his or her side of the story. Just as important, if the subject arrives at the interview unprepared to give you the information you want or need to know, the forewarning gives you license to press harder than you might have if you had not told the subject you needed some precise answers.

• **Empathize.** This is different from sympathy. Try to put yourself in the other person's shoes to understand how they must feel, their logic, allow them to define what they are saying. *Dateline NBC*'s John Larson says, "When interviewing someone about an emotional experience, do not interview about the emotion. Let emotion show naturally. Remember, don't do interviews; have conversations. If your story is about an empty factory, find someone—a janitor or the person who has to close it down. Ask that person to tell you about the 'ghosts,' the people who were once worked there."

• **Practice interviewing.** John Sawatsky recommends that journalists tape record their interviews and transcribe them to examine how

---

[6]Ibid., 53

they ask questions and to see which questions elicit the most useful answers. Become a student of great interviewing, just as journalists study writing and storytelling techniques.

INTERVIEWING RELUCTANT SOURCES

Journalists often encounter people at the worse moment of their lives. A person may have lost a loved one in an accident, lost a house and everything he or she owns in a fire, or might have been the victim of a horrible crime. The journalist's job is to find ways to tell the story without causing more undue harm. Despite what the public might think, most journalists I know hate to approach people who are in pain and ask for an interview.

But Sue Carter, an associate journalism professor who coordinated the Michigan State University Victims and the Media Program, says, "It is sometimes the *duty* of the reporter to offer the person the chance to say yes or no to an interview. Many people will not want to be interviewed—some may well scream or even become abusive when approached by a reporter. But your goal should be to provide those who want to talk the opportunity to do so, and that means explaining to them the mission or rationale for talking with you."

Carter says the mission includes:

- **Warn the community of the danger.** Victims, family, and friends may be willing to be interviewed when they understand that this provides an opportunity to help others avoid victimization.
- **Tell their side.** There are times when a victim may want to put his or her version on the record—the warning light wasn't flashing, the attacker threatened to kill her if she called police. Many victims complain that initial articles contained glaring errors of fact that they were never given the opportunity to correct at the time.
- **Illustrate an important issue.** As the culture tries to grapple with issues of violence—on the street, in homes, and at the workplace—the stories of victims help us understand the dynamics that allow such problems to persist. Remember, however, that victims of violence often feel guilty. The

domestic violence victim feels shame because she didn't leave. The rape victim thinks she should have known the man she was dating would turn violent. You are not violating your oath of objectivity to assure such victims that it was the perpetrator and not the victim who was at fault.

BE SENSITIVE, BE PREPARED

The best storytellers I know are tough and smart, but they also show caring compassion in their work. They show sensitivity for people who have been affected adversely by news coverage. They use special care when they interview children or others who are inexperienced in dealing with the media.

Journalists who covered the school violence at Columbine, the bombing of the Murrah Federal Building in Oklahoma City, and the attacks on the World Trade Center and Pentagon have learned important lessons about how to professionally and sensitively interview people in grief. A couple of days after the September 11, 2001, attacks on the World Trade Center, The Poynter Institute's Ethics Group Leader Bob Steele and I wrote an article for Poynter.org to help journalists who would have to approach grieving families and ask for interviews.

Telling Victims' Stories

By Al Tompkins and Bob Steele, The Poynter Institute

The victims of Tuesday's terrorism have names and faces. Slowly, we are learning the "who" behind the overwhelming images of disaster.

The dead include mothers and fathers, sons and daughters, friends, and famous names. They are business executives, a ballet dancer, retirees on their way to see loved ones, and working people who were taking long overdue vacations. They were ordinary people trapped in hijacked airliners and exploding skyscrapers. They were military personnel working inside this country's symbol of military might, and firefighters rushing to save lives in the twin towers of Gotham.

Just about every community in this nation will, in some way, be touched by the deaths of so many. Journalists take on the task of trying to learn all they can about who died and how they lived.

"When it works, you end up with this amazing story of humanity," says Jacqui Banaszynski, assistant managing editor of *The Seattle Times.* "Individuals who stand out as no one else, yet a collective of who we are as a community, country, people, world."

"The hard reality about such massive disasters is that names are the news...the heart of it," says Banaszynski, who guided the *Times*'s coverage of the Alaska Airlines Flight 261 crash in early 1999.

"Names and faces make the victims real and individual. They let us—force us—to look at them and touch them, know them. They show us what's now missing from our collective lives."

Banaszynski says she encourages reporters and editors to "mine for information" about the victims of a disaster. Find information "that brings the person back to life for a bit. Not just what they did, but what they did that made them who they truly were. Search for the personality as much as the pedigree. What marked them as special or unique."

Joyce Reed, vice president of news and marketing at KWTV-TV, Oklahoma City, learned valuable lessons about disaster coverage while leading her newsroom's coverage of the bombing of the Murrah Federal Building, in which 168 people died.

Reed says journalists must show concern for the vulnerable. "These ordeals are such public events that families need to have some control over how the general public remembers their loved ones."

Reed says it is important for families to have input about if or whether victims' pictures are shown. "Because an individual dies in a public fashion does not mean the family loses control over the loved one's memory. In the Oklahoma City case, all media outlets had the same picture of the individual."

Sometimes, Reed says, families approached news media asking them to air pictures of missing people. "Right after the bombing when people were missing, loved ones would bring pictures to us and say, 'Put this on the air in case somebody has seen my loved one.' But we did not go out and knock on doors."

Banaszynski says "timing and treatment" are the keys to dealing with victims' families and deciding what photos and information to use in stories.

"At some point they seem to want to talk. They want a chance to bring their loved one back again for a moment, to put words and memories to that life. People in grief are locked in a stage of remembering. I seldom find them loathe to share those memories if approached with sincere openness and sensitivity and professionalism."

Journalists take on a significant obligation when they talk with family members of disaster victims. "They desperately want information about their loved one to be right," Banaszynski says. "Often the doorway to getting a richer profile of a disaster victim is the simple but journalistically essential effort to get obituary information right."

When so many people die, it is inevitable that some of the dead will not have led perfect, unblemished lives. It was true in the Oklahoma bombing story. Joyce Reed said her newsroom chose not to include unflattering information in people's biographical stories. Reporters told the stories of how families wanted their loved ones to be remembered.

"Somebody would say, 'Maybe so-and-so had done X-Y-Z during their life.' It doesn't matter; that is not why they died. It has nothing to do with the blast," Reed says.

"I would advise journalists to go cautiously about reporting the unflattering details of somebody's life. Unless the details have something to do with why they died, I would leave it out. Don't cause more harm to already grieving families for no good reason."

Jacqui Banaszynski says it is "a hard call" when deciding what information to use about people that is "negative and [of] questionable relevance to the sum of their lives." The public criticized *The Seattle Times*—and the paper was critical of itself—in the handling of a profile of a victim in the Alaska Airlines crash. That story included information about a victim's connection to a crime from many years earlier.

Banaszynski says the lesson in that case was clear, and it applies to all other stories about victims. "Remember you are publishing what are likely to be the last words ever recorded in a public record about a person—and the first, in many cases."

"What is the important legacy of that person's life? What can you say just because you know it to be true? And what should you say because it is more truly their life?"

GUIDELINES FOR DEALING WITH FAMILIES OF VICTIMS

We all know reporters and photojournalists who seem to have a knack for landing interviews with people who tell others they don't want to talk to the media. There are plenty of tactics great reporters use to gather information from reluctant sources.

• **Clearly identify yourself as a journalist when dealing with grieving families.** Do not deceive to gain access.

• **Know what you are going to say.** Before you pick up the telephone or knock on the door make a mental note of the points you want to make and words or issues to avoid. Be direct in your approach, especially if the potential source is impatient or wants to leave. Practice your pitch in the shower and on the way to the interview. This is a skill just as writing and photojournalism are skills you can develop with practice. Develop contingency plans if sources turn away from you. Try appealing to their sense of fairness. Convince them that this is their opportunity to set the record straight. For example, you might say:

"I just want to get your side of the story." Or "I know there may be an explanation for what looks pretty damning here." You can appeal to their sense of public duty by saying, "If nobody speaks out or helps get the real truth out there, more people may be harmed."

• **Identify yourself.** Be sure the source knows to whom he or she is talking right away. This is not the time to be tricky or sneaky. Establish trust from the start, and it will serve you later when you start pressing hard for answers to tough questions. Make sure those you are interviewing know the purpose of your questions. Do not offer favors or gifts to families in order to gain access. I especially dislike the practice of sending flowers or food baskets to reluctant sources you want to interview. It gets dangerously close to paying for interviews, which most thoughtful newsrooms forbid.

• **Have a business card ready** with a short note explaining who you are, what you want, and how to contact you at your office, by cell, and at home. You will need this note and card if a source flatly says he or she is unwilling to talk or if nobody is at the location. Notes can be especially helpful when you are seeking information or an interview from somebody who is in deep pain at the moment. Sources may not want to talk to you, and you don't want to disturb them. But well-written notes can open doors. It is difficult to write such a note standing on the steps with the door closed in your face. Write it beforehand and have it ready if you need it.

• **First impressions.** If you are dealing with a reluctant source, it is often best to leave the microphone, camera, and lights in the car at first. Talk to the subject first without a camera. If appropriate, wear casual clothes. Keep your notebook in your pocket for a little while so you don't scare the source. Then, when you start writing notes, explain that you are just writing down some details that you don't want to forget when you get back to the office. I used to say something like, "I am getting too old to trust my memory, so I need to write things down— does that ever happen to you, you forget names or numbers?" Often the subject would say "yes," see that I am human, and warm up. You might offer a business card and assure the person that you can be reached if the interviewee needs to correct any factual mistakes he or she makes while talking with you, or needs to talk more later. You are not handing over editorial control of the story. The source must be clear that you and your colleagues, not the source, will edit the story. If a person allowed me into his or her home or told me important private details I usually gave that person my cell phone, direct line at the TV station, and often my home phone number. I have never had an unlisted phone number because I always wanted sources to be able to reach me. Reluctant sources need to know you are after the truth, not just a "gotchya" soundbite.

• **Discuss ground rules.** After you explain the purpose of the story, provide your honest estimate of the time required for the interview. If appropriate, offer a suggestion about the place, and ask for other suggestions. Tell sources how to let you know if they need a break, if they want the lights turned off, or how to talk about what remarks they want to avoid making. Journalists should be sure their sources understand that the reporter wants as much information as possible on the record. Everybody involved should be clear about what each side means when they use the terms "on background" or "not for attribution." Depending on how experienced the source is in dealing with the media, the reporter may have an obligation to help the source understand the potential outcomes of participation, including being fired from his or her job, making others angry, or becoming well-known by viewers. Journalists who have these discussions at the front end, before the interview, avoid haggling over whether they can or can't use part of an interview after the source says something newsworthy and then wants to be left out of the story. Make sure that victims know you are there as a reporter, not as their friend, but that your goal is to help them tell their stories—and tell them the way that they want to. Do all you can to avoid a dual-relationship as a friend and a journalist. The best thing journalists can do to help people in trouble is to tell the story honestly and clearly.

• **Protect sources, especially confidential or reluctant sources.** This is a legal as well as an ethical issue. Be careful about inadvertently burning a confidential source by carelessly giving out the source's name or business card. Don't leave the information lying on your desk or visible to others in your notes.

• **Avoid the Eddie Haskell approach.** Do you remember how, on *Leave It to Beaver*, Eddie was a jerk, but when Mrs. Cleaver came around Eddie turned syrupy sweet? The minute she was gone, he would turn into his old hateful self. Former *Los Angeles Times* investigative reporter Victor Merina says reporters should "be themselves." "If being themselves is not very nice," Victor says, "be nicer than yourself." Sources see through insincerity and can spot a fake a mile away. In the end, most sources will talk with you because they like you or because they believe you can help them.

• **Try the "you're not alone" approach.** Victor says one of the most powerful tools a reporter has is if he or she can honestly say, "I am talking with other people about this, too." Without revealing names of other sources, unless you have permission, indicate to the reluctant source that you are only getting a portion of the story from this source. With the help of this person and others, you can piece the entire story together. Without them, the story might lack context and not be fair.

• **Make sure the family has been notified.** The one assignment I hated above all others is when I would be told to go out to talk with family members who had lost a loved one in an accident, war, or some other tragedy. Even when you have official assurances that notification of death or serious injury has taken place; remember that, in today's world of fractured families, you might inadvertently be the bearer of this news to someone who has not yet been told. Always plan in advance what you will say and do if that happens. Have a plan for follow-up verification and try to make sure that the person is not left alone while you help sort out what happened.

• If this is the story about a death, **ask families how they want their loved ones to be remembered.** Sometimes families welcome the opportunity to take control over which photographs are used. Ensure that any photographs you receive are returned to the family as quickly as possible and in good condition. Go cautiously when considering whether to include biographical information about a victim that might cast that person in a negative light. Ask yourself whether that information is essential and relevant to the story. How public was the person? How widely known is the potentially negative information? Why does the public need to know that detail of the person's life?

• **Alternatives and other sources.** Who (other than a reporter) could act as an intermediary with grieving families to ask if family members would be willing to do interviews and/or supply background information and photographs of the victims?

If the source is unwilling to talk, ask if there are other family members, clergy, friends, neighbors, or co-workers who could talk knowledgeably. Even if the source you wanted grants an interview, don't forget to ask for a list of others who should speak as well.

• **Thank them for their time and effort.** Reliving a trauma takes a toll. Tell victims how much you appreciate their willingness to share their stories with you. Sources who you have carefully nurtured don't want to feel abandoned or used by you. Call up every now and then to see how they are doing. Get to know the source's family names and important dates in their life. Send an anniversary or birthday card if it is appropriate. Take time to get to know the "whole person," not just the part of the person who can help you in your job.

INTERVIEWING JUVENILES AND OTHER VULNERABLE PEOPLE

I have seen the toughest, most experienced journalists struggle when they have to interview children. Every TV reporter has experienced children who are far more interested in how microphones and cameras work than answering a journalist's questions. Kids don't care that you are smart, famous, and aggressive. Kids focus most on how they think you feel about them.

Journalists should talk with and interview children more often. Some of the nation's most vital stories revolve around kids:

- The Children's Defense Fund says children represent one-fifth of Americans who suffer from hunger. Sixteen percent of all children in the United States live in poverty. In fact in every state, children are more likely than adults to be poor.[7]
- The Department of Health and Human Services says more than a half-million American children live in foster care. More than 100,000 kids enter the system each year.[8]
- More than a thousand children a year die of neglect and/or abuse each year in America.[9]
- More children die from abuse and neglect than die each year than from drowning (850), heart disease (843), accidental gun injuries (110), poisonings (seventy), and falls (seventy).[10]

---

[7]"New Data Show High Poverty Levels for Children in Every State," Children's Defense Fund press release, August 6, 2001.

[8]"Adoption and Foster Care Analysis and Reporting System," U.S. Department of Health and Human Services, 2000. The data is presented for Federal Fiscal Year 1999 (FY99) which extends from October 1, 1998–September 30, 1999.

[9]"Child Maltreatment 1999," U.S. Department of Health and Human Services. These government estimates are based on responses from the states to the 1999 National Child Abuse and Neglect Reporting System (NCANDS). Data were collected in aggregate through the Summary Data Component Survey or at the case level through the Detailed Case Data Component of NCANDS.

[10]"Death by firearms ranks low in the U.S.," Jon E. Dougherty Worldnetdaily, February 5, 2000; "10 Leading Causes of Death, United States 1998, all races, both sexes ages 1–18," National Center for Health Statistics Vital Statistics System.

- Since the 1990s, legislators across the country have been changing state laws to allow ever-younger children—some as young as ten or eleven—to be charged with adult crimes. Prosecutors are waving more children than ever into adult court. Wardens are dealing with the aftermath by housing children with hardened criminals in adult prisons. By the end of 1997, more than forty states allowed the release or publication of certain juvenile offenders' names and photographs, according to the National Center for Juvenile Justice. Thirty states now allow open juvenile court hearings for certain violent crimes.[11] There are plenty of lobbying groups that say they work for kids. Every politician tells prospective voters, "Our kids come first." But you can re-read the bullet points on these pages and know that is just not true. Journalists who do not find ways to interview and understand children overlook the single most vulnerable group of people living in their viewing area.

But there are lots of reasons journalists don't interview kids. It's not just an issue of knowing how to ask questions in a way that a child will answer. Journalists must develop protocols for interviewing and identifying children. Those guidelines can free journalists to pursue stories they might otherwise avoid. (Remember, the first job of a journalist is to tell stories. "Seek truths and tell them as fully as possible.") But interviewing young people raises some of the most challenging questions faced by journalists.

Especially in breaking-news situations, juveniles may not be able to recognize the ramifications of what they say to others. Journalists should be especially careful in interviewing juveniles live, because such coverage is more difficult to control and edit. Juveniles should be given greater privacy protection than adults.

The journalist must weigh the journalistic duty of "seeking truths and reporting them as fully as possible" against the need to minimize any harm that might come to a juvenile in the collection of information. When interviewing juveniles, journalists should consider:

---

[11]"The Children's Beat: Reporting on Social Issues in America," *Newsletter of the Casey Journalism Center for Children and Families* (Winter 2000): 8.

What is my journalistic purpose in interviewing this juvenile?

- In what light will this person be shown? What is his or her understanding or ability to understand how viewers or listeners might perceive the interview? How mature is this juvenile? How aware is the young person of the ramifications of his or her comments?
- What motivations does the juvenile have in cooperating with this interview?
- How do you know what this young person says is true? How much of what this young person says does he or she know first-hand? How able is he or she to put the information into context? Do others, including adults, know the same information? How can you corroborate the juvenile's information?
- How clearly have you identified yourself as a reporter to the juvenile?

Minimize harm

- What harm can you cause by asking questions or taking pictures of the juvenile, even if the journalist never includes the interview or pictures in a story?
- How would you react if you were the parent of this child? What would your concerns be and how would you want to be included in the decision about whether the child is included in a news story?
- How can you include a parent or guardian in the decision to interview a juvenile? What effort has the journalist made to secure parental permission for the child to be included in a news story? Is it possible to have the parent/guardian present during the course of the interview? What are the parents' motivations for allowing the child to be interviewed? Are there legal issues you should consider, such as the legal age of consent of your state?

  If you conclude that parental consent is not required, at least give the child your business card so the parents can contact you if they have an objection to the interview being used.

Explore alternatives

- What alternatives can you use instead of interviewing a child on camera?
- What are the potential consequences of this person's comments, short term and long term?
- What rules or guidelines does your news organization have about interviewing juveniles? Do those guidelines change if the juvenile is a suspect in a crime and not a victim? What protocols should your newsroom consider for live coverage that could involve juveniles?
- How would you justify your decision to include this juvenile in your story to your newsroom, to viewers or listeners, to the juvenile's parents?

The Golden Rule for interviewing children

"Do unto other people's kids as you would have other people do unto your kids."

A FEW INTERVIEWING "DON'TS"

- **Avoid any hint of blackmail or coercion.** Especially when you are reporting about juveniles. Do not apply undue pressure on victims to cooperate with you. Never say, "Tell me about your daughter or I will be forced to get my information elsewhere."
- **Avoid talking about other sources or bad-mouthing people.** Victor Merina warns, "You don't know where this source's loyalties lie. If you start bad-mouthing other people, the source will wonder if you will do the same thing when the source is not around."
- **Watch what you say at the scene.** Reporters, like other first responders such as police and emergency medical personnel, sometimes indulge in black humor to cope with their own trauma. The danger, of course, is that family and friends could overhear those insensitive remarks and that could easily cost you an interview (and the witnesses' respect for you and your news organization).

REMEMBER: Focus your questions. Short questions, which focus on one point, are better than long double-barreled questions. Ask tough questions, not tough-sounding questions. Go slowly and gently with reluctant sources. Show special sensitivity toward juveniles, crime victims, and other vulnerable sources, but do not avoid them as potential interviews.

SOUNDS AND SILENCE

Besides interview sound, the other vital sounds on television are the natural sounds that photojournalists hear while they are recording images. One of the fastest ways to improve your storytelling is to dramatically increase the amount and quality of sound in your stories. Great stories about fires and firefighters include breaks to allow the viewer to hear the water rushing out of the hoses. They allow the viewer to hear the crackle of the fire. Great stories allow the viewer to listen as a roof caves in or a firefighter yells frantically for more water pressure.

I am talking about meaningful sound, not ambient noise. I promote the use of natural sound that enhances the viewer's understanding and doesn't just break up the copy in the story. Sound is best used when the sound is closest to the action. Consider these two sentences:

- Sixty million gallons of water rushed through the building (sound of water swooshing).
- Sixty million gallons of water (swoosh) rushed through the building (swoosh).

The second example gives the viewer twice as much water swooshing. More important, the sound of the water is near the first mention of the water. The sound authenticates the picture. It lets the viewer know exactly how close to the water we are standing.

Mark Anderson, the chief photojournalist at KSTP-TV, Minneapolis, once put a microphone on a dog to capture the dog's panting. By placing the microphone on the dog, he also captured the jingle of the tags on the dog's collar. Les Rose, a CBS news photojournalist, says when you use a mic in such an unusual way, remember that microphones are to be heard, not seen. If viewers start noticing the mechanics of the story, including the editing and equipment, they start "watching TV," not "watching a story." There is a big difference.

Reporters should learn to be quiet when a photojournalist is trying to capture great sound. Too often my photojournalist partners would send me a glaring look when they were trying to capture an image and sound but could not hear the chirping birds or the roaring jet because I was standing nearby talking with someone.

Honor those photojournalists who bust their humps capturing crisp sound by specifically writing that sound into the stories. Be precise when you script natural sound. Tell the editor *exactly what sound and shot* you are thinking of. In my experience, reporters who honor a partner's hard work tend to get a greater effort from that partner more often.

WORKING WITH MICROPHONES

The biggest mistake journalists make in capturing sound is they do not get close enough with a microphone. Reporters should become fanatical about great sound. There simply is no excuse for not having crisp, clear sound from news conferences and controlled interviews.

The three most important questions to consider in collecting sound are:

- How much noise is competing with the sound I want to record?
- How close can I get with the microphone?
- Is wireless a possibility?

If you are working in a noisy environment, such as a factory, a mall crowded with holiday shoppers, or an interview with a highway worker on a busy interstate, you are going to need a "directional" microphone. These microphones have a hotspot in just one direction, usually straight off the end of the mic. Shotgun microphones usually are best for those kinds of interviews. The photojournalist can take the mic off the camera and get it as close as possible to the interviewee or sound.

A lavalier microphone (most often cardiod or multi-directional in pattern) will pick up noises from many directions.

Of course, the crew should do all it can to minimize background noises, such as fans, blowers, and other sounds that compete with what you are trying to record.

There is no substitute for getting to a news conference a little early to be sure that mult-boxes work when you plug into them. If you are placing a mic on a speakers' stand, get the microphone close to the speaker's mouth. I have worked with plenty of photojournalists who insist we can get great sound by just sticking a mic near a loudspeaker. It almost never works. The sound is overdriven, muffled, tinny or, worse, full of feedback. It is a lazy way of gathering sound.

I do not know of any local news stations who use professional sound-men on their crews anymore. Even networks are not assigning sound-men to field crews. It means reporters and field producers need to work even harder to help the photojournalist capture great sound by carrying a wireless microphone. They must do everything they can to get that microphone close to the action.

BUILD IN SILENCE

Great television writing is not a gabfest. It is not wall-to-wall talking and soundbites. Take a few seconds to allow the story to breathe. Write silence.

This is a powerful tool because the world quite clearly is becoming a louder place. Viewers rarely experience silence on television. To many television journalists, it may sound odd to include silence in stories. But it is a technique as old as the first motion pictures. Silence builds suspense, creates space, and pulls the viewer deeper into the scene. Edward R. Murrow's "Christmas in Korea" opened with the sound of a shovel pinging against the frozen ground. But there was a second or so delay between the pings—a frozen, lonely silence that was not filled with other soldiers talking or laughing. We knew that soldier was out there alone, digging. We could see the shovel hit the ground, but the sound told us the tundra was impossibly frozen. Sound and silence work together to authenticate the pictures.

In stories that are dense with copy or in newscasts where one fifteen-second story follows another, a short break in the reading to allow a voice-over story to breathe can be so stark that it attracts viewers back to the screen. Viewers are busy while they watch TV. They are helping their kids with homework, they are cooking dinner, they are talking on the phone while the news is on. When the news goes silent, even for a couple of seconds, it breaks the pattern of noise and asks viewers to come back to the story with their full attention. This idea of building breaks in the action is not unique to TV. Symphonies and even rock songs use rests, breaks, and delays to build power and emotion.

To test the power of silence, start talking to someone, stop for a couple of seconds, then start again. You will see the listener pay closer attention after the pause.

This principle of building in silence is just as important for twenty-second voice-overs that the anchors read with video as it is to longer stories full of drama and tension. In fact, a few seconds of well-placed silence builds drama and tension in what are otherwise flat, ordinary stories. Allow the viewer to wait a second or two while a judge prepares to read a verdict. Allow an ambulance to rush through the screen. Write an anchor pause into the script; allow the story to take a breath.

REMEMBER: Silence can be a powerful storytelling tool. It can draw viewers back into a story, give them time to digest information before you move on to the next point and even add suspense and drama to a story. Newscasts don't have to be gabfests. It takes discipline to be quiet and allow stories to unfold in pictures and sound, as well as words.

Chapter 7

Shoot for the Eye

"If I could tell a story in words, I wouldn't have to lug a camera."
LEWIS HINE, INVESTIGATIVE PHOTOGRAPHER*

PICTURES ARE THE MAIN POWER of television because pictures convey immediacy, intimacy, understanding, and emotion.

We assume that "seeing is believing." It would be logical to assume that the brain accurately records the scene that the eye observes. And yet that is not true. Eyewitnesses to violent crime are notoriously unreliable when it comes to giving descriptions of the criminals, and yet there is no doubt they saw something. In 2000, WCPO-TV, Cincinnati, investigative reporter Laure Quinlivan produced a remarkable story about misidentification of criminal suspects. She said that about half of all eyewitness reports prove to be false. And she reported that when a weapon is involved in a crime, witnesses are able to give a far more accurate description of the weapon than of the person holding the weapon. Experts told her that if the victim is of a different race or ethnicity than the criminal, the reliability of the eyewitnesses to recount what happens gets shakier still. So, *seeing* is not to be believed.

Just because we see it, does not make *it* the truth. It makes it *our* truth. The brain's understanding of any visual scene gets filtered through the viewer's wide range of emotions and experiences. On top of that, the viewer's perceptions may be altered by the photographic and/or editing techniques that journalists can use.

Boston College professor Ann Marie Seward Barry cites a study by the Educational Foundation of the American Association of Advertising

---

*Lewis Hine (1874–1940) is best known for his photos of immigrants at Ellis Island and for pictures of children being forced to work, which led to new labor laws.

Agencies which shows that even when we see images on television, we usually don't understand them. Barry writes, "Even when we watch television, *we misunderstand approximately 30 percent of what is shown to us.* Our emotional state, our mindset at the time, and our experience all seem to conspire against our seeing things as they really are. We go about our lives, however, mostly assuming that what we see really 'is,' as if there were no intermediary process—in other words, as if the map were indeed the territory."[1]

There is no doubt, Professor Barry says, that visual communication dominates verbal communication. It is a powerful notion for television journalists to consider. The power of pictures and sound overwhelm the words they cover. Yet in my experience, few reporters and even fewer producers have any formal training in understanding the principles of photography or graphic design.

This chapter will:

◇   Explain the main principles of great photojournalism storytelling.

◇   Explore ways to make words, sounds, and pictures work together, rather than compete for the viewer's attention.

◇   Explain how to think visually when designing graphics for television.

LET'S GET VISUAL

Pictures tell stories. Cavemen told stories with pictures, elaborate stories about the day's hunt or an encounter with a bear, without ever scratching down a word. They drew pictures on the walls of caves that told stories so clearly that centuries later a grade school child could decipher the tale, just through the pictures. But television photojournalism takes those pictures and adds sound, sequencing, and movement. The cave drawings told stories one frame at a time. TV tells stories thirty frames per second.

The best television stories get *close-up* to help the viewer feel, taste, smell, and see the story. And they get *wide,* to give the viewer a context and perspective of the scene.

---

[1] Ann Marie Seward Barry, *Visual Intelligence* (Albany: State University of New York Press, 1997), 16.

Mark Anderson is the chief photojournalist at KSTP-TV, Minneapolis, and is a former National Press Photographers Association (NPPA) Photojournalist of the Year. He pressures himself to include a variety of shots and visual sequences in his stories. "I want every story to have wide, medium, close-up, and super close-up shots," he says.

By editing the individual shots into sequences of actions, one action leading to another, the story gets a "flow."

An Action Without a Reaction Is Only Half an Action

Photojournalists and reporters are drawn to action as a moth is attracted to a flame. When you arrive at a breaking news scene, a good rule of thumb is to "shoot what will go away first." In other words, immediately shoot the fire, shoot the rescue work, shoot the action. But Anderson says it is also important for photojournalists to not just "face the action and shoot it," but to "turn your back on the action to see the *reaction* to the action."

"That is where you will see the faces of the firemen, the scenes of horror, and fright of the people who are losing their homes to the fire," Anderson says. "You will never see the emotional reaction to anything if you only face the action. Turn your back on it."

Les Rose, the photojournalist for the popular CBS News series *Everybody Has a Story* with Steve Hartman, says TV photojournalists should "always be thinking about the tape editor. While I am shooting, I try to give ourselves as many options as possible once we get into the edit booth. I think, 'If there were five cameras shooting this live, what camera shot would a director punch up next?' I ask myself constantly, 'Am I capturing the moment?'"

Rose says the photojournalist is 85 percent psychologist and 15 percent photographer. "A big part of my job is to predict what people will do. If you are just shooting the moment, you will miss what comes next. If, for example, you are photographing a child eating an ice cream cone on a summer day, you should be alert to the idea that the ice cream might melt and fall out of the cone. When it begins to fall, you would get in close. Then, you would anticipate that the child might start crying, so you would not wait until she yells to move in on her face. If you wait until she yells, you have missed the shot. Once the scream leaves her mouth, be alert to the parent who will come to her rescue with a napkin and a hug."

Some photojournalists would shoot the sequence of events as one long action. The best photojournalists would see the dropping ice cream as an action followed by a series of reactions: surprise, crying, and compassion. Les sees the shots, not just as a sequence, but as an unfolding story—a drama. Photojournalists who do not *anticipate* reaction have little influence over their images; they just shoot what is before them. But photojournalists who anticipate action and reaction can make crucial decisions about framing, focal length, and background before the shot even presents itself.

Rose says the reaction shot, more than the action shot, is what the viewer relates to. When a football player catches a ball and runs for a touchdown, the crowd cheers. The crowd is doing exactly what the viewer at home might do—reacting to the great catch. The viewer identifies more with the crowd—the reaction—than with the player, which is the action. Sometimes, great photojournalists make the action and reaction part of the same shot. Action and reaction do not always have to be portrayed in separate shots cut together. Great photojournalists might record the touchdown pass, follow the player across the goal line, and then pan up to the crowd as the player spikes the ball in the end zone. It is all one fluid shot, action and reaction. It is less jarring than two or three edited shots. And the viewer gets a more authentic sense of what it was like to be there because there is no edit between the action and reaction.

Once reporters and producers learn the importance of reaction shots, they become far more tolerant of the times when photojournalists do not seem to be "shooting the good stuff." Producers begin to edit video differently. I only wish I had learned this lesson earlier in my career. Many times, as a reporter, I said, or at least thought to myself, "Hey, turn around—you're missing it," when my photojournalist partner was shooting the reaction shot. How many times producers or editors cut together a story composed of action shot after action shot without ever putting in a reaction to the action. No wonder the story is difficult for the viewer to follow. No wonder viewers understand so little of what they see on TV.

If a photojournalist never shoots reaction shots, coach them to do so. Reporters can help photojournalists anticipate what action will come next by being an extra set of eyes and ears. This "lookout" function can be especially important if the action is about to take place on the right side of the camera. TV photographers have one blind spot, and it is on the right side. While a photojournalist is looking through a viewfinder, the camera blocks the right side. The reporter should protect that side and be alert to images and actions the photojournalist can't see without looking away from the viewfinder.

INVISIBLE AND INFLUENTIAL

The best photojournalists I have worked with are stealthy in big crowds. They move quickly and quietly around their subjects. They do all they can to make the camera, microphone, and lights as invisible as possible. They know that the less attention they draw to the camera, the more natural the subjects are likely to be in front of it. Great photojournalists show children how the camera gear works in order to demystify it. Most kids get tired of it all and go back to being normal pretty quickly.

In interviews, great photojournalists do all they can to make their subjects bored with the camera and other gear. They try to make it all just seem mechanical, uninteresting, and part of the woodwork. The first pictures that great photojournalists usually take are of the subject doing some mundane activity, not usually the most important photographic moment they anticipate happening that day. There is a reason. They want the subject to be comfortable with the camera before the big moments, the "money shots," unfold.

The best photojournalists I have worked with helped shape the stories they were working on; they were not content to just shoot the pictures. They offered ideas to develop the story, and they offered questions to ask the people we interviewed. After reporters ask the who, what, when, where, and why questions, great photojournalists can sometimes ask the "heart and soul" questions that the subject might answer. It is not unusual for interview subjects to talk more freely to the photojournalist, the "regular Joe in blue jeans" than the reporter who is wearing a suit and tie. Photojournalists are journalists who use a camera instead of a notebook or a word processor.

The best photojournalists appreciated it when I asked questions to learn more about their craft. I tried hard to learn the language of photojournalism, not just to tell stronger stories, but as a way for me to show respect for the photojournalists I worked with, elbow to elbow, every day.

Just as there are theories about what makes writing clear and strong, there are important theories about why some images and graphics are more effective in communicating clear and memorable messages.

> REMEMBER: Viewers may misunderstand one-third of everything they see on television. The most powerful and memorable images on television often are not action shots, but images where people are reacting to the action. Great photojournalists are more than "shooters" or cameramen, they are journalists who carry a camera.

A LITTLE BIT OF VISUAL THEORY

How is it that viewers misunderstand a third of what they see on TV? The answer may lie in how viewers process the images they see. Once you understand the theory behind how we process images, you can begin to form your own ideas about how to more effectively tell stories through pictures and graphics.

Gestalt psychology, a term derived from the German term *gestalten* or organized wholes, is a theory of perception. I offer a short exploration of visual perception to help you understand the power and potential for television visuals, including photographic images, graphics, and animation.

Perceptual psychology aims to find out how we attach and derive meaningful symbols from the simple electrical impulses that make us aware of light, dark, and color in our visual systems. You may have taken one of those ink blot tests when you were in grade school, or maybe you have seen psychologists or psychiatrists administering perception tests in the movies to see if somebody is psychotic. What those tests really measure is how you associate visual images with your personal experiences.

While vision goes on between the eye and the brain, perception is a process entirely within the mind. And, as we discussed earlier, the mind filters the perception through prior experiences and emotions.

Look at the Gestalt illustration on the next page. What do you see?

Some people see two faces in silhouette. Some see a vase or chalice.

Gestalt theory maintains that the mind has innate organizational abilities that allow us to deconstruct a whole image into various compo-

nents without having to actively analyze them. So you can see one, then the other—the faces, then the vase—without much thought about either.

THE BIG PICTURE

The guiding principle of Gestalt psychology is that the larger picture will be seen before its component parts. This has particular relevance for the television news and is effectively the psychological equivalent of the old saying, "The whole is bigger than the sum of its parts." It is why Mark Anderson's rule of shooting "wide, medium, close-up, super-close-up" is so important. If the storyteller only used one shot, for example, our perception of the scene would be based on one "whole." But break the story into component parts (using different focal lengths and angles) and we begin to understand the scene more fully. Varying shots allow the brain to analyze the story from many points of view.

Probably the most important Gestalt concept is the theory that, in any visual display, there is always one object that will be perceived as the object. Everything else is perceived as background. In television, we clutter our screens with information we think will be appealing to the viewer. In fact, the brain is not able to process so much information.

Gestalt theory probably would suggest that CNN *Headline News'* complex design of box upon box of information, coupled with changing headlines and throbbing music, is too much for the viewer to comprehend. Viewers, Gestalt theory might hold, would focus on one main object and put everything else in the background.

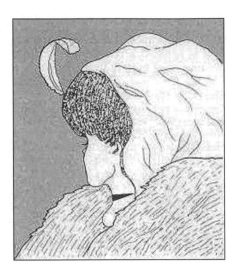

What do you see in this image first published in 1888? Some see the provocative picture of a young woman turned away from the reader. But others see an old woman. The old woman's nose is the young woman's chin. The young woman's ear is the old woman's eye. When you focus on one main image, the rest falls in the background. You cannot see both images at the same time.

The Web site Illusionworks.com notes, "This (image) illustrates once more that vision is an active process that attempts to make sense of incoming information. Perception is the construction of a description." So it is with television news. The descriptions that accompany video and graphic illustrations build the viewer's perception.

SEEING WHAT WE WANT TO SEE

The second guiding principle of Gestalt psychology is that when there are a number of possible interpretations, we automatically choose the one for which we need the least amount of additional information. It is a way of saying, "The viewer will see what he/she wants to see." If a newscast aired a story in which demonstrators were chanting anti-government slogans, my father might have seen that story as being "anti-American." I might see the same story as being a demonstration of the power of protected free speech. We all filter stories through our own experiences, and we turn first to the interpretation we understand most. We choose the interpretation that is the most obvious to our own eyes and brain.

VISUAL VERSUS VERBAL

Gestalt theory has profound importance for politicians who show up on the news. They often stand in front of American flags, surround themselves with children, or make certain that decorated war veterans are at their side as they speak at political rallies. CBS *60 Minutes* correspondent Lesley Stahl talked about this in a 1989 Bill Moyers/PBS documentary *Illusions of News.*[2]

Stahl said, "We just didn't get the enormity of the visual impact over the verbal. It was a White House official who finally told me.... I did a piece where I was quite negative about (President) Reagan, yet the pictures were terrific—and I thought they'd be mad at me. But they weren't. They loved it and the official outright said to me, 'They didn't hear you. They didn't hear what you said. They only saw those pictures.' And what he really meant was it's the visual impact that overrides the verbal."

There is no point in a reporter or anchor reading copy when he or she is trying to compete with an overwhelming image. If the video in the story is the space shuttle exploding, the Concorde blazing down the runway, or a hijacked airliner slamming into the World Trade Center, stop reading when that image comes up; let the image soak in.

"Researchers tell us that negative images wipe out what viewers hear in the audio track of a TV story," says Deborah Potter, executive director of Newslab, a Washington, D.C.–based news laboratory that helps local stations tell more effective stories. "If a viewer is watching an emotional and negative piece of video like a plane bursting into flames and crashing, they are not listening much. They are processing the image."

I remember watching a story on CNN right after the July 25, 2000 Air France Concorde crash. The anchor was reading a story about the remarkable safety record of that aircraft, but the video the network used to cover the anchor copy was of the jet with flames shooting out its rear end. I could not hear the story about how safe the airplane was through history because the remarkable pictures transfixed me.

---

[2]*The Public Mind: Image and Reality with Bill Moyers*

REMEMBER: The eye looks for the larger picture before it looks at its component parts or secondary images. The eye sees one main object in any picture or image and everything else is secondary. When there are a number of possible interpretations of an image, the viewer automatically chooses the one that requires the least new information.

THE POWER OF THE PICTURE

Photojournalism has the power to influence foreign policy and even military actions. If there ever was a doubt about the power of television pictures on world opinion, that doubt evaporated after Saddam Hussein invaded Kuwait in August 1990.

A few minutes after I picked my daughter up from day care January 16, 1991, the Allied bombing of Baghdad began. I sat in my newsroom office in Nashville, Tennessee, watching as CNN's Bernard Shaw, Peter Arnett, and John Holliman described the stunning pictures of missiles exploding and Iraqi guns throwing up flack. At the same moment, British Prime Minister Margaret Thatcher watched the coverage in Britain, Russian President Boris Yeltsin watched in Moscow, and President George Bush watched the war he just ordered unfold on his television set. In her book *Lights, Camera, War*, Johanna Neuman writes, "Even Libya's Muamar Qadafi watched the CNN coverage from his tent in Tripoli, calling CNN's control room in the days before the war to say he had a plan to resolve the conflict peacefully. Staffers assumed he was a crackpot and hung up. There simply was no precedent for this experience. This was real-time war."[3]

Sometimes a single still photographic image holds the most power over human emotion. *Washington Post* media critic Tom Shales concluded that "shocking and heartbreaking TV pictures of starving children in Somalia helped motivate the American response to send troops to that country."[4]

---

[3]Johanna Neuman, *Lights, Camera, War* (New York: St. Martin's Press, 1996), 212.
[4]Tom Shales, "Looking Forward, Looking Back," *The Washington Post*, December 27, 1992, sec. G, p. 1.

For ten years, Americans barely noticed as more than a million Somalis had died of starvation, disease, and civil war. In 1991 and 1992, CNN aired fourteen separate stories on the growing desperation in Somalia and Sudan.[5] It was not until TV and newspapers showed the one image of a baby girl dying of starvation while a vulture sat a few feet away from her that Americans put a face on the starvation and intervened with what the administration called a "humanitarian effort." Late December, 1992, 10,000 soldiers were on their way to Somalia.

But the mission that started with humanitarian intentions turned ugly less than a year later, October 3, 1993 as seventy-five U.S. Army Rangers and forty Delta Force troops in seventeen helicopters began searching for lieutenants to Somali "warlord" General Mohamed Farah Aidid. The search went bad, and Somalis shot two Army Blackhawk helicopters out of the sky. The Somalis captured one soldier, a Blackhawk pilot, who was part of the 160th U.S. Army Division, the secret special operations regiment known as the Nightstalkers. They were based at Fort Campbell, an hour's drive from our television station in Nashville.

A WSMV-TV reporter, Annette Nole, confirmed that the captive solider was Michael Durant. We learned that his wife and eleven-month-old son lived in our viewing area.

By the next day, the Somalis released a videotape of Durant. His face was swollen and bloody. He could barely speak. "You kill people innocent," the interviewer insisted. "Innocent people being killed is not good," is all Durant would mutter in return.

The power of that short videotape set the nation on edge. CNN, then the only twenty-four-hour cable network, played the tape endlessly. Then television delivered the next round of pictures. *The Toronto Star*'s photojournalist/reporter Paul Watson witnessed Somalis mutilating soldiers' bodies. Television networks picked up the newspaper's still pictures of Somalis dragging one of the bodies through the streets of Mogadishu and jubilant Somalis jumping on the downed helicopter's rotorblades.

The heartbreaking and gruesome photos of the dead and of Mike Durant covered newspapers and newsmagazines, and ran endlessly on television. Florida Rep. Luis Gutierrez spoke for many when he said that he turned against the U.S. intervention in Somalia because "The pictures caused me great pain and consternation, as I'm sure they did to every American."

---

[5]Neuman, *Lights, Camera, War*, 229.

October 14, 1993 the Somalis released Durant after eleven hellish days. The pictures of his release signaled the beginning of the end of America's involvement in Somalia. Americans could not get out of there fast enough. On Christmas Eve, only six weeks later, I stood on a Fort Campbell tarmac, the same place where Durant had come home to a hero's welcome a few weeks earlier. I was covering the arrival of one of the last airlifts of soldiers who served in Somalia. (See "Soldier Comes Home," Chapter One, pp. 9–11.) America's involvement started when photographs of starving children pierced the hearts of American viewers who felt they could not stand by and watch a nation starve. A year later, photographs of American servicemen battered, imprisoned, and dead led to the end of the war.

Professor David Perlmutter called this power of news photography on foreign policy "the CNN effect."[6]

The picture of a young man standing in front of a Chinese tank in Tiananmen Square prompted Rep. Nancy Pelosi (D-Calif.) to proclaim, "We have an opportunity in this chamber to stand with that man for democracy."

Even President George Bush, upon seeing that video, said, "I was so moved today by the bravery of that individual that stood alone in front of the tanks rolling down the main avenue there. And I'll tell you, it was very moving. And all I can say to him, wherever he might be or to people around the world, is we are and we must stand with him."

Later, *Time* magazine reported (January 6, 1992) that White House spokesman Marlin Fitzwater said the administration's first response "was based almost entirely on what we were seeing on television."

Simple images crystallize the public consciousness about complex events. Those images include Joe Rosenthal's 1945 photo (*Old Glory goes up Mount Suribachi*); Charles Moore's 1963 photo (*Attack dogs on Civil Rights demonstrators, Birmingham*); John Paul Filo's 1970 photo (*Girl screaming over dead body at Kent State*); and Nick (Huynh) Ut's haunting 1972 picture (*Naked little girl and other children fleeing napalm strike*).[7]

Seven months after the picture of screaming Phan Thi Kim Phuc, a nine-year-old Vietnamese girl, was published in *Life* magazine, the United States moved toward a peace agreement. The *Los Angeles Times*, seventeen years later, said that image of an agonizing little girl "with

---

[6]David Perlmutter, *Photojournalism and Foreign Policy; Icons of Outrage in International Crises* (Westport, CT: Praeger Series in Political Communication, 1998), 5.

[7]Adapted from Perlmutter, *Photojournalism and Foreign Policy; Icons of Outrage in International Crises.*

its anti-war theme, flashed around the world, came to symbolize, more than any other photograph taken in Vietnam, the atrocity of war."

In almost every one of these examples, the reaction to the action gives the picture great strength. The Kent State photo is not a picture of a soldier shooting; it is a student grieving over and reacting to the shooting. The napalm strike photo did not show the action, but the reaction to it. I do not remember one *action* shot from the 1980 Winter Olympics of a hockey player scoring a goal. But I can vividly picture the reaction of young American hockey players winning the gold medal.

That reaction to the action explains why some images, whether still or video, reach the heart through the eye. The viewers can relate to something they hold important in their own lives. It may be the reason a picture of one agonizing little girl can move public opinion against the war even after years of coverage of shooting and bombing did not. Television photography, unlike the visual media of painting or sculpture, does not rely a person to interpret a setting in order to capture it. To be sure, the photojournalist can influence our understanding or reaction to an image in a myriad of ways, but what he or she records is an unaltered truth. It is up to the viewer to interpret it.

Seeing, for many viewers, is believing. But to really "understand" requires explanation and context. That is a key role journalists fill.

Pictures and Words Should not Match

Some of my reporter and photographer friends will see this statement and wonder whether I have lost my marbles. For decades, reporters have been taught that words and pictures should match. I thought so too, until my photojournalist partner Pat Slattery, chief of photography at WSMV-TV, taught me not to "say dog, see dog." It took me awhile to understand his well-placed point.

He meant, "Don't mention a dog if you are showing a picture of him. Talk about the dog being man's best friend, talk about the dog saving a child's life, tell me the dog's name or something about him, but don't tell me it is a dog. I can see that."

It was a profound lesson in writing and storytelling. I had always believed that words, pictures, and sound should "match" on TV. Pat taught me that words should *explain* the pictures. The words should tell viewers something they would not know about the pictures, even if they were standing next to the photojournalist when the pictures were taken. You have learned in this chapter that when words and pictures compete, the pictures win. But when they work together, the images do not overwhelm the words, the words make the pictures even more powerful and meaningful.

Think about how an expert would lead you on a tour through an art museum. She would not point to a famous picture and tell you, "That picture has a gold frame." You could see that. You don't need a museum guide to tell you that. It is very much like writing "dog" when you are showing a "dog" in a news story.

If the art expert wanted to be helpful, she might tell you, "The painter was angry when he painted this picture, which is why he used short, choppy strokes." Now you might understand something you would not have known even if you and the expert were standing side by side looking at the same picture. A journalist, like an art expert, should add meaning to the viewers' understanding of what they see.

CBS correspondent Steve Hartman told me, "I never write a sentence without knowing what pictures go along with it." Hartman becomes a guide for the viewers to understand not just what they are looking at in his stories but to understand what they do not see on TV. Poynter's senior scholar, Roy Peter Clark, encourages writers to imagine the difference between "*placing* the viewer in a scene and *pointing* to the scene." Taking the viewer to the scene means acting as a guide or an interpreter. Pointing to a story is akin to driving by a car accident and saying, "Look at that." It calls attention to the scene but adds no real meaning. Writing to the pictures is just telling the viewer "what" is on the screen. But writing to the edges of the pictures, writing about the pictures, now that is telling me, "So what? What does it mean? Why does it matter?"

My colleague at The Poynter Institute, Jill Geisler, says, "Words and pictures should hold hands." They should not compete with each other and they should not be redundant. The words help viewers understand the pictures.

In the "1030 Morgan" story (Chapter Two, pp. 21–25), Boyd Huppert did not "narrate" the pictures. The words and pictures held hands. For example, when a fire hose that was showering the dust of the demolition created a rainbow, Boyd *did not* write, "Then, a firehouse sprayed water to keep down the dust. The sunlight hit the water and formed a rainbow, and several people noticed it."

That would have been say-dog see-dog writing. Instead, Boyd wrote:

> BOYD: Yet, out of the dust, the mist, and the sun came
> a symbol.
> NEIGHBOR NUMBER FIVE: Do you see the rainbow?
> Yea.
> BOYD: A sign of hope.

Boyd allows the viewer to understand the pictures by experiencing them. He tells the viewer something about the rainbow; it is a sign of hope. The pictures tell the viewer "what." The copy tells the viewer "what about that."

Former NBC correspondent and anchor Linda Ellerbee wrote about her discovery that writers should write *"with* television, letting picture tell story. To explain, let me suggest an experiment. Turn on the newscast and go into the next room. Now, listen to any story on the newscast—from beginning to end. If the story is perfectly clear to you at all times; it is a normal newscast. There is a name for this manner of telling a story. It's called radio. If it's television, you will be unable to stay in the other room and still get it all. If it's television, it will compel you to watch. At least it should; if it doesn't, throw out your television and get a radio."[8]

GIVE VIEWERS A SENSE OF PASSAGE OF TIME IN YOUR STORIES

If viewers are to feel they know the heart of a character, the writer must give the viewers the sense that they have passed some time with the character. Try to show the character in more than one scene, more than one situation.

I know that many television journalists are desperately pressed for time when they are shooting stories. That makes it all the more important that, when they start shooting, they know they need the main characters to be in more than one physical scene. I am not suggesting you spend more time interviewing. I do urge you to interview the main subject of your story in at least two settings. One setting is a more formal sit-down interview using a tripod-steadied shot. This setting is

---

[8]Linda Ellerbee, *And So It Goes* (New York: G.P. Putnam's Sons, 1986), 85.

particularly good for those questions that require deep thinking and analysis. It is the "what" part of the story. The second main interview is "off the shoulder" with the camera moving as the subject is in a more relaxed setting. The off-the-shoulder interview is more relaxed, does not include the distraction of TV lights and often elicits the best heart-felt soundbites; the emotional part of the story.

This word of caution: If you ask a story subject to do something in front of the camera, be sure the viewer knows you asked the person to do that. Let's suppose we are telling the story of an old Army vet who did something heroic on this day fifty years ago. We have very little time to shoot the story, very little file tape, and no time to go get other war buddies. It is just him, and we have to have this piece on in a few hours. How can we make the story look full and seem as though we passed some time with the subject?

It is completely acceptable to say, "We asked him to show us the yellowing photographs of his Army life. He keeps those memories stuffed in a cardboard box on the third shelf of his hall closet. The old photos are starting to fade with time, but his memories of Charlie Company are as clear as the day he snapped this picture."

To maximize the moment, don't ask your subject to gather some pictures before you get there. Go with the subject to the hallway closet, rolling on everything. Get close up on the door handle as he opens the door. Get him turning on the light switch to the closet. Get him grunting as he reaches into the closet. Get the pictures and sound of him bringing down the box and opening the cardboard lid. Capture those first seconds of him shuffling through the photos looking for just the right one. You know he will say something like, "Oh, here is one I won't forget." This is *great* video and sound that would cover a couple of paragraphs of track easily. Just as important, it gives the viewer a sense that you spent some time with this guy and that you know him. The feel of the story will be far different than if you just interview him on the sofa and cut to some static still pictures.

Even in news conferences, try to talk with the main subject before he or she begins an official speech. Ask him or her what would make this a really good day, a really useful news conference? Press for the subjective reasons for even holding this news conference. What were the arguments in favor of or against making an announcement here and now? During the news conference look for symbols that time has passed; people tiring, people checking their watches, the speaker's water glass emptying, TV crews packing up and going away, the banners and bunting coming down, the janitors moving in. Even when others stop shooting at the end of an event, keep shooting to capture the nuances that others will not notice.

REMEMBER: Show the main character(s) in more than one setting. Those extra visual dimensions give viewers the feeling that they have spent more time with the character. The viewers are more likely to have feelings for the characters if they feel they know them.

CAUTION, THIS MAY GET GRAPHIC

When I was a news director, there were few comments that could draw my ire as quickly as when someone said, "That is not a TV story; that is a story for newspapers."

It was as if there were some stories that were so complex that they could not be told clearly and interestingly on television. It seems to me that what the person usually meant was, "We don't have any visual way of telling that story well on television."

I want to spend a few pages helping you think through what makes really effective graphics work for television. The goal is not to make you a graphics expert or graphics artist, but to give you a language and appreciation for the power and potential of graphics in stories.

THINK "SHAPES"

Think about all of the shapes we respond to without a second thought. If a stop sign didn't include the word "stop" on it, we would still recognize it. Drivers know they should slow down when they see a yellow sign with an image of school children on it. In airplanes, people of many languages and cultures universally understand the "buckle the seatbelt" and "no-smoking signs." When I was working in South Africa, I saw this sign (shown on the following page) and marveled at how little explanation I needed to understand that I should be very careful driving on this road.

The sign served as fair warning that unless I drove carefully I might have a hippo bouncing off my car's front grill.

My big breakthrough in thinking about graphics came from a one-sentence utterance from a newscast producer, now a special projects executive producer at WTVJ-TV, Miami. Teresa Nazario said the secret to great graphics is "to think shapes, not numbers or words." It makes so much sense. With that great line of thinking as a launch pad, I drafted a checklist for reporters and producers to consider when they ask for or design television graphics:

• **Understand first, then be understood.** How clearly do you understand this story? Does the information make sense? Is it logical, believable, reliable? Do you know the source and/or motivation the source has for supplying the information? Understand the story completely before you try to design a graphic to go with the story. Vague understanding produces vague, or worse, confusing news graphics.

• **What is the context of this graphic?** If the story is about a rise in crime, for example, ask:

- Where is the rise occurring?
- How does this rise compare with the total crime pattern?
- What are the possible reasons for it?
- Who is most affected?
- Who is not at all affected?
- Who has the power to keep the system as it is?
- Who profits from the system staying as it is?

Consider this:

- Nicetown records fifty murders this year.
- Pleasantville records twenty-five murders this year.

Is Nicetown twice as dangerous as Pleasantville?
You would need more information, such as:

- Nicetown has a population of 200,000 people.
- Pleasantville has a population of 25,000 people.

So, you should ask, what is the ratio of murders to population?

- Nicetown's murder rate is 50/200,000 (or one in 4,000 people is murdered).
- Pleasantville's murder rate is 25/25,000 (or one in 1,000 people is murdered).

In fact, Pleasantville's murder rate is *four times higher* than Nicetown.

- **Ask more sophisticated questions to get better graphics.** Is a 100 percent increase in murder the result of one mass murder, or many acts in separate areas of town? Does the increase represent a significant increase in crime, or has the murder rate gone from one person killed per year to two killed this year? How could you show where crimes occur in your town? Most cities have crime pockets, not random crime that occurs everywhere.

With graphics and stronger information we could make routine stories about murders and robberies much clearer. By asking *where* the robberies occurred, not just how many robberies occurred, we could learn that forty-eight of the fifty robberies occurred in Nicetown's upper northeast side in a ten-block area.

Our graphic could show a map demonstrating where the robberies occurred.

Then we could ask *what* the robbers are hitting most often. We learn that forty-five of the forty-eight robberies involve liquor stores, and most of Nicetown's liquor stores are located in the upper northeast side. Suddenly, we understand the root of the city's robbery wave. Nicetown's police department needs to get more patrols around the liquor stores.

- **Go lightly on numbers.** Consider these:

1997	54
1998	63
1999	71

The numbers are simple but not effective as graphics. Your eye is trying to make mental calculations bouncing around the relative differences of the years first. The years and robberies represent different things (time and criminal incidents) yet they are represented by the same symbols— numbers. The eye sees and the brain decodes the difference in the second line of numbers. Back and forth, back and forth *up to twelve times* to absorb the entire graphic. The seven in 1997 is smaller than the eight in 1998, so you determine the years are increasing. But on the other side of the graphic, you see that the four, three, and one appear to be decreasing, but when you take into consideration the whole number, you see the number is increasing. It all gets so complex and the graphic is only on the screen for a matter of seconds. Remember, few viewers sit silently staring at the news like deer staring at car headlights. They are trying to take this information in while doing other things. No wonder viewers only understand a third of what they see on TV!

• **Be symbolic.** It is difficult to see the relative nature of numbers when they are presented quickly on the TV screen, but it is easy to understand a budget is growing when the bag of money on the screen is growing. Imagine you have no words—the graphic should be visual information that needs little or no verbal interpretation. How clearly would viewers understand what you are trying to show? Remember that numbers can be hard to read on a television from across the room. Symbols that replace numbers might be clearer.

Viewers have even more trouble visualizing big numbers. Kokogiak Media *(www.Kokogiak.com)* developed a Web site called the MegaPenny Project to help the public understand big numbers by using simply familiar objects. For example, if I asked you to imagine 1,000 pennies you could probably come up with a fairly accurate image.

1,000 Pennies

But what would 100,000 pennies look like?

100,000 Pennies

Now, try to imagine one million pennies. What if I told you it was a stack measuring five feet high by one foot thick. It might still be difficult for you to get an image in your mind. But when you see the picture, the graphic image, you understand right away how big a stack of one million pennies would be.

One Million Pennies

Now that we know what a million pennies look like, let's move into the billions. This is where we really start to lose our viewers. Think about it: Does an interstate bridge cost a million dollars or is it a billion dollars? What would be a reasonable guess? Most of us would not know where to begin. Seeing the difference between these two numbers might help.

Here is a stack of one billion pennies. Each block of pennies is the size of a school bus. If you were to stack these pennies in a single pile, the stack would reach one thousand miles.

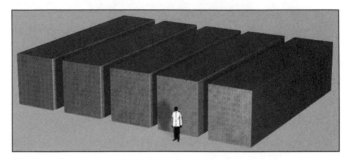

One Billion Pennies

Now let's move to the numbers of a mind-boggling size, the kinds that journalists toss around when they speak of state and federal budgets. How much space would ten billion pennies fill?

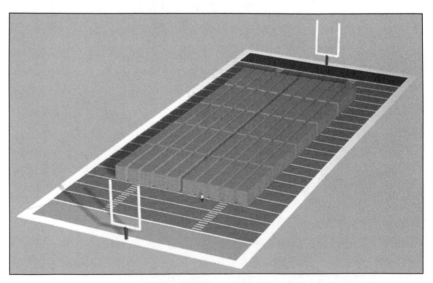

Ten Billion Pennies

Without the football field, the ten billion figure becomes too difficult to imagine.

Remember, viewers learn more quickly and deeply when they can
relate the information to their own experiences. Take a look at why this
next illustration does not mean as much, then let's see if we can find a
way to make it more meaningful. Here is a pile of one trillion pennies.

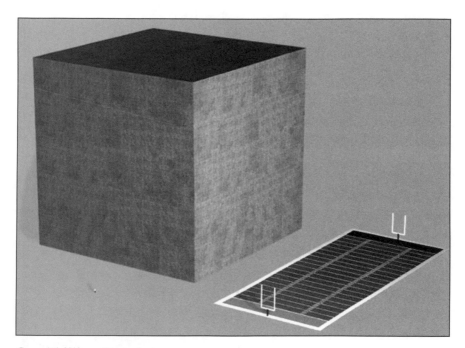

One Trillion Pennies

It is difficult to get a fix on the size of the cube. We can see its
length, but how tall is it? To understand its real mass, let's compare it to
something familiar that is also large and block-shaped. Now, you can
imagine how big the one trillion stack really is!

One Trillion Pennies

From right to left you see the football field, the Lincoln Memorial, the Washington Monument, then the cube of one trillion pennies, then the Empire State Building, and the Sears Tower. By the way, one trillion pennies is worth ten billion dollars.

But often in local television, there is not time for the graphics department to produce a graphic for your story. On weekends and early morning shifts, many newsrooms have no graphics support at all. At such times, think graphically. How could you find something of similar size or shape to the image you are trying to create in the viewer's mind?

John Barr and photojournalist Mark Anderson of KSTP-TV, Minneapolis, took this same penny idea and turned it into a news story. When the federal government was trying to figure out how to spend a $1,800,000,000,000 budget surplus, the team grabbed a folding table, two chairs, and a box full of glass Mason jars and sat down in a city park.

They spread 180 pennies on the table and asked people passing by to place the pennies in the Mason jars labeled "military spending," "education," "foreign aid," "entitlement programs," "welfare and social programs," and so on. As people allocated their pennies, they explained their decisions. An art student dumped fistfuls of pennies into the schools jar, a World War II veteran sank most of his pennies into a jar marked "defense spending." The pennies helped us understand much larger numbers. It was a way of thinking shapes, not numbers.

• **Think clearly about the focus of this graphic.** Don't tell the viewer anything that does not have to do with the story. Ask, "What *exactly* do I want the viewer to learn from this graphic?" You should be able to express the answer in one short sentence. You want viewers to see that the budget has doubled, or that rapes are occurring mostly within this five-block area of town.

• **Movement can be good, but...** The Nicetown robberies graphic could be effective if the line grows as you reveal the numbers. But be careful with movement. Make things grow or disappear in accurate proportion to the real life passage mentioned in the graphic. For example, if, over several years, lawmakers voted for a series of budget cuts for the police department, you might show a "fever line" moving slowly south. But if the number of crimes rose at the same time, be careful not to make the upward arrow shoot up too quickly. The video movement may make an inaccurate editorial statement. Make the growth proportional to the years that passed.

Remember that movement in the background of the graphic may be visually pleasing to the producer and/or the artist, but movement near or behind the main information of the graphic is, at the very least, lost on the viewer. Worse yet, the movement may draw attention to itself and away from the information you are trying to convey.

Spend less time worrying about how the graphic will play in the *newsroom* and more time worrying about how it will play in people's *living rooms*.

• **Write after you make the graphic,** not the other way around. This will assure the copy and graphic match exactly.

• **Ask others to look at the completed graphic.** Allow them to tell you what they understand the graphic to be saying. This process is no different and certainly no less important than copy editing.

• **Get it right! Demand as much accuracy in your graphics as you demand for your news copy and photojournalism.** Considering the power of the visual to communicate in ways the word cannot, there is a special need for numerical and graphic accuracy. So if you want to show crime has doubled in five years, your graphic should show a doubling by proportional growth. Graphic representation should be precision work, just as news writing should be precision work.

Monica Moses, a Poynter Institute expert in visual journalism and graphic design, says, "Never illustrate what you do not know to be true." Journalists would not attempt to tell stories in copy that they do not know to be true. The principle is no difference in visual journalism. Yet in the first days after Princess Diana's death, there were many conflicting graphic explanations of how the crash occurred. After the attack on the World Trade Center on September 11, 2001, many newsrooms developed animation and still graphics that explained how the buildings collapsed. But those graphics were trying to explain something that was still unclear. Did the collapses occur because of the weight of the aircraft in the buildings? Did the buildings collapse because the fire weakened the steel supports? What part of the collapses occurred because the crash sheared some superstructure supports? Engineers will investigate the collapses for years, but journalists scrambled to explain such complexities within hours of the attacks, and risked their credibility.

"It is easier for writers to write around ambiguities and holes in their stories," Moses said. "Writers use vague words like 'some,' 'many,' and 'often' when they do not have hard facts. But it is almost impossible to draw around what you don't know. That's why news graphics require journalistic precision."

Beyond the still "over the shoulder" and full-frame still-image graphics that television newscasts use routinely, many now use animation and moving images, which present new journalistic and ethics challenges. Monica Moses wrote about the issue for Poynter's Web site, *www.poynter.org*. "It's now technically possible to illustrate not just where planes struck the World Trade Center but to show their flight paths, the angle of impact, and the eventual implosion of the buildings."

Moses continues, "With the potential for movement come new challenges." For one still frame or over-the-shoulder image, a graphics journalist must render one scene accurately; for an animated graphic, he or she might have to get thirty scenes right for just one second of animation.

"That is a lot of visual information to report, confirm, and display," Moses says. "In the early days of newspaper infographics, a little 'illustrative license' was often accepted; now the rules for accuracy in graphics are as rigorous as those for text reporting. And while a writer may be able to 'write around' missing information in text, a graphics journalist can't 'draw around' murky details in a graphic."

"Animation is a hell of a tool," said South Florida *Sun-Sentinel* graphics director Don Wittekind, "but it brings new responsibilities." *The Sun-Sentinel* staff elected not to animate its September 11 graphic of the World Trade Center collapse because it didn't have enough information on precisely how the buildings fell.

Wittekind told Monica Moses that he and artist Scott Horner watched the ubiquitous TV clips of the implosions—and they saw animated graphics on the Web that depicted collapse. But they didn't feel comfortable using motion in their graphic.

"The buildings did not fall straight down," Wittekind said. "There was some tipping." But he and Horner couldn't be sure of the angle and precise timing of the collapse, so they didn't attempt to re-create it.

At *The Sun-Sentinel*, which produces some of the world's most sophisticated 3-D and animated graphics, the view is "Get it right, or don't do it," said Wittekind.

If an animator tried to illustrate the assassination of President Kennedy, for example, the animator would show how bullets entered and exited the president's body. It would show the trajectory of the shots. Those issues are the subject of heated political and historical debate even today. Besides issues of accuracy, there are questions about whether news consumers can handle the cold dissection of tragic events emotionally, even if such examination improves the public's understanding of important events.

Tone and a concern about authenticity were also factors in *The Sun-Sentinel*'s decision not to animate its WTC graphic. "We wanted to treat the event with respect," said Wittekind.

Dr. Mario Garcia, an online and print visual communication expert, has advice that translates well for television journalists who are trying to learn how to more effectively use graphics in their stories. "Visual journalists wear the hats of the writer and editor as they move through the progression of an assignment. Something that looks good but is difficult to comprehend fails to communicate information quickly and deters from the story. Graphics can be as complicated as stories. A good visual journalist knows that simplicity and elegance work best."

According to Garcia, the public is saying:

- "Please uncomplicate those graphics. I don't have all day to analyze statistics that you have to be an MBA recipient from Harvard to understand."

- "Put in those little touches that tell me if this is a happy or sad story. Show me mood."
- "Calculate that my time is reduced these days." Don't waste the viewer's time with graphics just for the sake of graphics. Just because your station bought a fancy new switcher or animation package does not mean your stories need to include graphics with images flying around in them. Ask yourself the question, "What is the best way to make this story clearer and more useful for the viewer?"
- "Beware that I am a visual animal, not by choice but by conditioning. I like to see things—the face of the politician or the corner intersection near my house where two cars collided. Show me."

Remember: Be certain you understand the information before you try to display it graphically. Think shapes, not numbers. Compare big numbers to something the viewer can visualize. If 70,000 people die each year from a disease, compare that to the number of people it would take to fill a football stadium, for example. Newsrooms should have the same standards for accuracy and context in graphics as they do for writing and photojournalism.

PHOTOGRAPHIC AND GRAPHIC OBJECTIVITY

There is no such thing as an objective photograph or graphic. Before we record, produce, or edit any image, the photojournalist, reporter, and producer make many decisions that affect the outcome. The nature of the news process edits out information. So every decision a photojournalist, producer, editor, or reporter makes is subjective, based on his or her own opinions, experience, and judgment about what is newsworthy and important. Beyond that, photojournalists and graphic designers make other decisions that can affect the viewer's perceptions:

• **The background:** CBS's Les Rose makes the point clearly. "If I am giving a speech and the nine U.S. Supreme Court justices are standing behind me, the speech certainly has one meaning. But if I am giving the same speech and the nine people standing behind me are Elvis impersonators, then the speech takes on a different meaning. That is how important the background is to an image."[9]

Political image-makers drape their candidate's stages with the American flag or enormous campaign banners bearing the candidate's name or likeness. Such an image makes the politician appear patriotic or larger than life. The photojournalist has a duty to keep the background authentic to the story.

Background colors portray strong emotional signals. Psychologists say that blue, green, and purple have "cooling" properties. Red, orange, and yellow are seen as "warm colors" with energy, stimulation, and a sense of urgency.

That is why many set designers use blues, purples, and greens in their sets while reserving the warmer colors for graphic designs. Most often, for example, stations choose red as the background for their "live" or "breaking news" banner supers. Red banners and backgrounds scream "urgency." But like "The Boy Who Cried Wolf," if the warm urgent colors are overused, the viewer gets desensitized to them and the colors begin to mean nothing.

• **The focal length of the lens:** It is completely possible for a photojournalist to shoot a room with five people in it and make the room appear crowded. By standing far away from the people and shooting them in a shallow depth of field, the image is compressed and the people seem to be crowded together. Even a beginning photographer can make a puddle look like a lake or turn a burning bush into a virtual forest fire.

• **The angle:** Associate Professor of Communication at Boston College, Ann Marie Seward Barry writes, "The language of camera angles is highly manipulative emotionally and is perhaps one of the simplest and easiest to understand examples of visual language grounded in perceptual experience."[10]

---

[9]Les Rose interviewed by the author November 2, 2001.
[10]Ann Marie Seward Barry, *Visual Intelligence* (Albany: State University of New York Press, 1997), 135.

By shooting a subject from a low angle, the subject takes on an image of power. Eye to eye, the subject and the viewer are on neutral territory in terms of power. On occasion, news directors have asked me why their anchors seem to lack "on-camera authority." Sometimes I find the anchor is actually looking up to the camera lens, making him or her appear weak.

Professor Barry observes, "In Nazi propaganda posters, the Aryan family, the Nazi soldiers, the worker in the field, the Hitler youth: all were shown from low angles and bathed in light and color. Likewise in the National Socialist Democratic Party children's books, German workers and officers are depicted in high angle and bright colors; Jews, however, are shown caricatured with dark complexions, ill-shaven and scowling; inevitably from a high angle and predominantly in black and white."[11] When setting up an interview, the journalist has to be aware of the subtle signals that the angle sends to the viewer.

• **Lighting:** Almost nothing can change the editorial tone of an image more than the lighting. Subjects shot in extreme dark light or deep shadows make them look evil or mysterious. Photojournalists who blast their subjects with bright Frezzi lights, or "sun guns" as they are called, may make the subject look guilty. Bright light often makes men look unshaven or skin appear to be spotted or splotchy. Dark light or shadows on the face can make an interview subject appear shady, evil, or untrustworthy. But shadows are important tools for giving images texture and definition.

Warm, even light may make interview subjects appear soft and friendly. CBS' Les Rose has a love for lighting. Rose told me, "If you want to light well, you have to first remove existing lights. Often that means getting rid of all of the light you did not construct yourself, such as lamps, overhead lights, and window light so that you can construct the photographic light." Les seats the reporter between the main key light and the camera. That puts the camera on the same side as the shadow on the subject's face. A second lesser light, would be on the other side of the camera filling in a bit of the shadow on the subject's face. A third light would highlight the interviewee's hair and shoulders from the back, giving separation from the background. If a fourth light can be added, it can be used to light the physical background to give it definition, texture or color.

Let's see what this would look like. (Photos used with permission from *www.Cybercollege.com/lighting.htm,* copyright Ron Whittaker 1996–2001.)

---

[11]Ibid., 136.

First, we remove all existing light in the room. Then let's add a back light on the subject's hair and shoulder, as Les Rose recommends. Right away, we add separation between the subject and the background.

It's time to add a key light. When the key light is on top of or is too close to the camera, we see the harsh look that is typical of so much spot news video. The straight-on light eliminates the background and washes away all of the nuances and textures that make the picture interesting. Kevin Johnson, a photojournalist at WVEC-TV, Norfolk, and editor of the popular photojournalists' Web site B-Roll.net, tells photojournalists on the run, "The worst lighting is direct light coming from the same angle as the lens; such as camera mounted lights. Straight-on light flattens out features and makes the subject too bright in relation to the background.

Look how much more pleasing the shot becomes when the key light moves to the left of the camera with the back light adding separation from the background. Suddenly, we get shadows that add texture and detail. Whenever possible, get the light off the camera. Reporters can do their photographic partners a huge favor by holding the portable light whenever possible.

Now add a fill light to the right of the camera. This is the classic three-light triangulated setup. Be careful not to let the fill light overpower the key. The fill should not erase the shadows, just fill some of them in to add definition and texture. Without the fill, we would not see the eyes on the man on the left. The robe on the man in the middle takes on new definition when we add a fill light. The main difference between professional photography and home movies is the quality of the lighting.

If you have a distracting or undesirable background, it might be a good idea to place the camera as far away from the interviewee as practical and zoom in. The zoom will force the depth of field to fall away and the background will become less noticeable.

Rose says if the photojournalist is in a hurry and can only string two lights, "Use the key light and the hair light."

The best lighting is when the viewer does not even notice the interview was lit. The lighting should never be more memorable than the subject.

• **Cropping and framing:** Depending on how the photojournalist frames a picture, scenes may appear close or far away, almost touching or separated by great space. Extremely close cropping of a picture may be wonderfully intimate or have the effect of an in-your-face Turkish prison inquisition.

• **Camera movement:** Camera movement gives a feeling of urgency and "being there." The movement gives the viewer a sense that this scene is not rehearsed. It is too unpredictable to set the camera on a tripod and get steady. Too much camera movement, or movement that is not inspired by on-the-screen action leaves the viewer feeling that the photojournalist is on a visual ride to nowhere. The viewer begins to focus more on the movement than on the visual and editorial content of the story.

WVEC's photojournalist Kevin Johnson says, "If you are going to move the camera [pan or tilt], there is no reason for the camera not to be on a stable platform." Johnson says, "Zoom with your feet, not with your lens. The human eye does not zoom, so your camera shot should not. Physically move the camera closer to the subject instead of zooming in."

Unnecessary camera movement is the hallmark of amateur photography. Go to an electronics store and watch people try out home video cameras. The first thing they do is pan and zoom endlessly. Camera movement should be a photographic tool, not a crutch.

• **Special effects:** Effects such as slow-motion or "drop-frame" of open shutter photography all affect the viewer's understanding and feeling about the image. There were times when I was a news director that I only half-jokingly threatened to put duct tape over all of the special effects buttons on our newsroom edit machines. Our newsroom, like many others, sometimes used the effects for no good journalistic reason. We used them because we could. I believe that when TV stations show slow-motion images of someone in handcuffs, it can makes that person look dangerous and guilty.

• **Music and sound effects:** In their book *The Elements of Journalism,* Bill Kovach and Tom Rosenstiel suggest one of the principles of journalism should be "Do not add." That means do not add something to the story that did not happen. Kovach and Rosenstiel write, "This goes further than never invent or make things up, for it also encompasses rearranging events in time or place or conflating (combining into one composite) characters or events. If a siren rang out during a TV story, and for dramatic effect it is moved from one scene to another, it has been added to that second place. What was once fact has become fiction."[12]

This kind of "audio sliding" has become both easy and common in television news, and it is a kind of deception that is invisible to the viewer. With the advent of digital editing, I have noticed a lot of television editors, photojournalists, and reporters "sliding audio" in stories. The editor takes a sound that occurred in one scene and edits it into a scene in which it did not exist in reality. Here is an example of this technique:

The photojournalist is taking pictures of a storm. The photojournalist gets great sound of the wind howling and rain pelting the street. A few minutes later, the photojournalist gets a great picture of trees bending in the wind, but the sound is no good, somebody nearby is hollering, a truck is passing by behind him. He decides to marry the great sound with the great picture in the edit booth.

This is an acceptable editing technique in some newsrooms. But The Poynter Institute's Chip Scanlan, warns against "reconstituting the truth" in editing. Scanlan says when journalists reassemble reality they have to take great care not to distort or mislead the viewers about what happened. For example, it would have been unacceptable for the editor to borrow some sound of a howling wind from a story he shot six months ago during another storm.

A good question to ask in such circumstances is what would the viewer say if he or she knew the truth about how this story was gathered and edited? Would the viewer feel deceived or tricked? When adding any sound or effect, it should be obvious and apparent to the viewer that the journalist has chosen to alter the scene or sound.

Rosenstiel and Kovach say, "Journalists should not deceive (the viewer). Fooling people is a form of lying and mocks the idea that jour-

---

[12]Bill Kovach and Tom Rosenstiel, *The Elements of Journalism* (New York: Crown Publishers, 2001), 79.

nalism is committed to truthfulness." This principle is closely related to "Do not add."

Kenny Irby, the group leader for visual journalism at The Poynter Institute, says, "Ask yourself, 'Is this what I saw through my viewfinder when I took the picture?'" If the photojournalist records music that occurred at the scene of their story, then that is ambient sound that might ethically be edited into the story. But if the music is a soundtrack audio recording, then the journalist must ask if the music adds an editorial tone to the story that would not be present without the music.

I learned a painful lesson about this when I was a reporter. Photojournalist Lyle Jackson and I had produced a powerful series of stories about the number of aging convicts who were piling up in prisons around the country. Inmates as old as seventy-five and eighty showed us their knee replacements, hip replacements, and one inmate showed us his scars from a recent bypass surgery. We watched state-run physical therapy sessions inside prisons for old convicts whose joints were getting too stiff to get out of bed. Some of the old guys needed special soft food because they had no teeth. A large percentage of them could not escape from prison if you left the front gate wide open. We wanted to raise the question of whether it made any sense to keep these seniors in prison at all.

One of the stories we produced included the inmate who had served more years in prison than anyone else in Tennessee. The old guy was moaning and groaning in the early morning air as he walked next to a razor wire fence. We added a little subtle piano music in the background. It was slow and soft as the prisoner's scatchy old voice rose above it, talking about all of his years at hard labor working in a prison cotton field. He had murdered another man in a barroom fight and escaped after he was sent to prison for that crime. Now he was an old man. It was a moving scene.

My own mother, who was watching the news that night, called me to complain. "Don't try to make me feel sorry for those convicts," she scolded me. "He is a murderer and murderers should be in prison," she ranted. (I should tell you, by the way, that my mother worked at a maximum security prison for more than twenty years.) I realized that it was the music that added a tone of sympathy to the story that the words and pictures did not convey.

• **Edit in context:** Viewers generally, I think, understand that television is a process of *editing out*. They are more confused about the choices we make about what we leave in stories.

Years ago, a press secretary for Jane Eskind, a powerful woman who was running for Tennessee governor, complained to me that it seemed my partner and I were constantly choosing to use video of Mrs. Eskind eating. There are very few things that are less flattering to a person's public image than to show that person eating all the time. Candidates often wolf down their meals because they are in a hurry to make a speech or shake more hands or try to get in a few bites before somebody interrupts them again. It is not a pretty sight.

From that point forward, for the rest of the campaign, my partner, Mike Todd, and I made extra efforts to edit around the "eating video" as a matter of fairness. But we also avoided the "eating pictures" because we worried that viewers might not hear a word I was saying in the story if they were obsessing over images of "that woman who is eating again."

That is the central lesson of this chapter. Pictures and graphic images hold great power. In his book *On Bended Knee, the Press and the Reagan Presidency*, writer Mark Hertsgaard quoted ABC News' Sam Donaldson as saying, "A simple truism about television; the eye always predominates over the ear when there is a fundamental clash between the two."[13]

That simple truism explains why men watching NFL football can't hear their wives trying to talk to them, why my son can't hear me while his eyes are radar-locked on *Dragon Ball Z* cartoons, and why the news viewer can't hear the reporter explain the long history of safety that an airliner has had because the station is showing pictures of a plane crash.

Television images change the course of human history. TV images have the power to ignite wars and civil uprisings, inspire peace movements, and prompt legislative action. There may be no more powerful tool known to man. The moving image may, in the course of time, prove to be as significant as the evolution of the wheel, or the invention of gunpowder, the moveable type printing press, electricity, the combustion engine, and the microchip were. Television aims directly at the viewer's heart when the storyteller uses the Holy Trinity of tools at his or her disposal; words, pictures, and sounds.

---

[13]Mark Hertsgaard, *On Bended Knee, the Press and the Reagan Presidency* (New York: Farrar Straus Giroux, 1988), 25.

REMEMBER: When the eye and the ear compete, the eye wins. Journalists have a responsibility to ensure that they honestly and accurately present images and sounds in the context of what really happened. Journalists should resist using audio and visual editing effects that might skew the viewer's understanding or perception of an event or issue. Focal length, lighting, background, and framing all may reflect the photojournalists' own biases about the subject. Journalists should recognize their own biases and find ways to report around them.

Chapter 8

Tough Calls on Deadline—Ethics and Broadcast Journalists

"And ye shall know the truth, and the truth shall set you free."

ST. JOHN 8:32

IT WAS A CHILLY MARYLAND evening on March 5, 1999. I remember the sting of the frosty night air in my lungs. If I had been a drinking man, I might have ended up in a bar that night. Instead, I chose a walk in the brisk air to clear my mind. I had just facilitated a focus group with a roomful of Baltimore residents who had been recruited to represent an entire broadcast market. They were young, old, black, white, Latino, rich, poor, working class, and students. The group confronted me with disturbing questions and opinions about how TV reporters and producers do the work of journalism.

I was not the only one who left the meeting a little bit stunned. The group was assembled so broadcast journalists could listen to the concerns of everyday viewers. I asked the public to talk and to tell the truth as frankly and clearly as they could. I asked the journalists to say nothing, just to listen and learn all they could from their viewers. The residents spent an entire evening talking about everything from crime coverage to investigative reporting.

Nearing the close of almost two hours of discussion, I told the group members that we were profoundly grateful for their participation. I told them that my Poynter Institute colleague Dr. Bob Steele and I, along with the Radio-Television News Directors Foundation (RTNDF), were attempting to write a series of guidelines. We hoped to help broadcasters think through how they should cover issues such as identifying juveniles, covering stories live, and covering tough-to-tell stories such as suicide. Then, someone asked the question I didn't expect.

121

"Do you people have any standards?" a Baltimore CPA asked that roomful of journalists. For a few moments, two dozen journalists were silent. "How could somebody not know how seriously journalists take this issue of ethics?" we all wondered. But the journalists also knew there is wide disagreement about what those journalistic standards for ethical conduct should include.

Jeffrey Pollack, the accountant, was not trying to be condescending or mean-spirited. He and others in the room were expressing their concerns about broadcast journalism.

Their opinions reflected the findings of the 1998 RTNDF national survey. Viewers in the survey said they are "more skeptical about what they see on TV lately." They strongly believe that ratings, personal bias, and the desire to "get the story first" motivate journalists. They are not alone. According to both viewers and news directors, the bottom lines for local news stations are ratings and timeliness. Eighty-seven percent of news directors and 92 percent of the public say news reporting on local TV is often or sometimes improperly influenced by the desire to increase TV ratings. An equal percentage (91 percent) of viewers and news directors agree that reporting is improperly influenced by the desire to report the story first.

Viewers question the use of confidential sources, undercover cameras, and violent and graphic images. And they question the effects of competition and business values on the news. Another survey, by the American Society of Newspaper Editors (ASNE), found that half of the adults questioned believe that "TV is worried more about profits than the public interest."

Each year the Gallup Organization polls Americans about which professions have the highest standards for honesty and ethics. In 1997, out of twenty-six professions measured, TV reporters ranked twelfth. Journalists' ethics ranked below funeral directors and dentists, but a few positions above local politicians and building contractors.[1]

By 1999, TV reporters ranked twenty-fifth on the list of the most ethical professions. More than one out of four respondents said the profession's ethics were either low or very low. Auto mechanics and nursing home operators rated higher than TV journalists. TV

---

[1]"Honesty and Ethics Poll: Pharmacists strengthen their position as the most high rated occupation," December 13, 1997, Leslie McAneny and Lydia Saad, Gallup News Service.

reporters barely edged out labor union leaders (thirtieth) and lawyers (thirty-seventh).[2]

No other profession that Gallup measures has lost more ground with the public. The pollster says, "The three professions that have lost the most in the ratings (of high or very high) over the last ten years are:

1) TV reporters, down from 32 percent to 20 percent

2) Lawyers, down from 22 percent to 13 percent

3) Congressmen, down from 20 percent to 11 percent"[3]

What can journalists do about our tarnished public image? Diane McFarlin, the publisher of the *Sarasota Herald-Tribune* (and former chair of the ASNE Ethics and Values Committee) suggests, "Explaining our policies and judgments would go a long way toward increasing public trust in the press."[4]

We should be able to explain, first to ourselves and then to our newsrooms and viewers, why we do what we do. We must be up-front and honest about our journalistic mission and our motives, including ratings, awards, self-promotion, business pressures, and legal concerns.

The most difficult time to establish policies and make ethical decisions is when you are faced with a deadline. Guidelines, protocols, and decisions that newsrooms discuss front-end, off deadline, are almost always more reasoned than decisions that journalists make in the heat of a competitive deadline battle. So, I encourage you to discuss these issues now. Articulate your newsroom's standards and be prepared to stick to them in a moment of crisis. You will eliminate confusion in the newsroom and restore credibility with your viewers.

In this chapter, I will explore:

◇ What Poynter's Bob Steele calls "The Guiding Principles for Decision-making in Journalism" and how to put them in practice.

◇ Guidelines for journalists to evaluate the sources they use.

---

[2]"Nurses displace pharmacists at top of expanded honesty and ethics poll," November 16, 1999, Leslie McAneny, Gallup News Service.

[3]Ibid.

[4]"Perspectives of the Public and the Press; examining our credibility," The American Society of Newspaper Editors, 1999.

◇ Criteria for when and how confidential sources should be included in coverage.

◇ The use of graphic images and words.

◇ Covering, interviewing, and identifying juveniles in news stories.

◇ Guidelines for thinking about the issue of invading privacy and interviewing vulnerable people. When and how should journalists invade privacy?

◇ Some ideas about how to ethically cover "breaking news" live on the air.

SETTING STANDARDS

In 1999, I was teaching an ethics seminar in South Carolina. I had presented a series of case studies in which journalists had made tough and sometimes controversial decisions in stories that involved juveniles and sexual abuse. One student marched up to me when we took a break in the class and demanded to know, "Are you saying there is no right or wrong answer? Is there no truth? Are you saying that every journalist has to make his or her own decision without any rules to go by?" It reminded me of that accountant in Baltimore: "Don't you people have any standards?"

But then I had what, for me, became an important insight. We should have standards, guidelines, and protocols to go by. The participant in South Carolina was demanding inflexible and rigid *rules* for coverage. I want to make an argument that journalists should establish thoughtful guidelines for coverage but resist the temptation to write a lot of rules that may limit their ability to report important stories.

So in this chapter I will offer some guidelines that your newsroom might adopt, amend, or improve. Many of the guidelines I wrote in collaboration with Steele, whom I consider to be the nation's leading thinker on media ethics issues. I can't prove it, but I suspect I would not be challenged when I suggest that Steele has taught more ethics seminars to more professional journalists than anyone else in America during the last decade and a half. The Society of Professional Journalists and the Radio-Television News Directors Association adopted a considerable amount of Steele's thinking and writing into their national codes of ethics.

For more than a decade, Steele has used three main concepts as his guiding principles for ethical decision-making:

GUIDING PRINCIPLES FOR THE JOURNALIST

Seek Truth and Report it as Fully as Possible

- Inform yourself continuously so you in turn can inform, engage, and educate the public in a clear and compelling way on significant issues.
- Be honest, fair, and courageous in gathering, reporting, and interpreting accurate information.
- Give voice to the voiceless.
- Hold the powerful accountable.

Act Independently

- Guard vigorously the essential stewardship role a free press plays in an open society.
- Seek out and disseminate competing perspectives without being unduly influenced by those who would use their power or position counter to the public interest.
- Remain free of associations and activities that may compromise your integrity or damage your credibility.
- Recognize that good ethical decisions require individual responsibility enriched by collaborative efforts.

Minimize Harm

- Be compassionate for those affected by your actions.
- Treat sources, subjects, and colleagues as human beings deserving of respect, not merely as means to your journalistic ends.
- Recognize that gathering and reporting information may cause harm or discomfort, but balance those negatives by choosing alternatives that maximize your goal of truthtelling.

IN PURSUIT OF THE TRUTH

Where should journalists go to find truths? Every decision a journalist makes while reporting influences the truth he or she might find. I suggest these guidelines:

   • **Be thorough.** How do you choose to whom you talk, or not talk? How many voices and points of view should you include in your reporting? What was your motivation for talking to some people and excluding others? What truths could others have given you that might have added perspective to your investigation?

   In the workshops and seminars I teach around the country, many journalists tell me that they consider it their job to "tell both sides of a story." I urge them to find more voices than "both sides." I struggle to find even one story that has only two sides. Let's look at the issue of the death penalty. A list of those who have a stake or interest in this issue includes:

   • The condemned prisoner
   • The victim(s)
   • The family of the victim(s)
   • The prisoner's family
   • Anti-death penalty groups
   • Pro-death penalty groups
   • Prosecutors
   • Defense attorneys
   • Lawmakers/politicians
   • Judges
   • Juries
   • The wardens
   • All other death-row prisoners
   • All other inmates
   • All other crime victims
   • Society at large

   What a rich list of stakeholders, and it is just the beginning. Yet we have to admit that few of these stakeholders ever make it into the news. Great journalists seek truths through many voices with many points of view, especially those whose voices are seldom heard.

   • **Be accountable to the public.** This does not mean that the public's views should guide journalists. We should be guided by the principles of our news organization, principles that should include seeking the truth and telling it as fully as possible. But we should be *informed* by the views, morals, and values of our community. If you were doing a story about segregation, for example, it would be crucial to know how various parts of your community feel about the issue. But even if the majority favored legal segregation, your journalism should not be swayed by that; your journalism should be guided by the need to seek the views of as many voices as possible, including those in the minority who are being discriminated against.

• **Set the story in context.** Great stories include both intimate examples and wider content to show the size of the issue. It is possible to be "accurate" but not true. If you have no context for the action, you still have not captured the truth.

For example, let's suppose you went undercover investigating "dirty restaurants" and found a food worker touching his or her hair then preparing food. You also record undercover images of food prep workers touching raw meat, then not washing their hands before touching other food they are preparing. You notice some dented cans in the pantry, and you see that the refrigerator thermometer is broken. Do you have the proof you need to expose this restaurant as unhealthy and dangerous? What if, on closer inspection, you found that the restaurant had a long history of excellent inspections? Not one person is known to have ever gotten sick at that restaurant. In fact, the restaurant owner was one of the first organizers of a voluntary food workers' education program sponsored by the local restaurant association.

The pictures you recorded were accurate, but they do not reflect how seriously the restaurant tries to comply with health rules.

Journalists should provide context in their stories. They should go beyond the question of "what" and explain "why," "how often," and "who is responsible."

• **Seek contrary evidence.** Did you put as much effort into disproving the allegations as you did in proving them? Great investigators stay open to the idea their original information is not accurate. They do *not* believe everyone is a crook or a liar. Great investigators are neither cynical not gullible. How hard did you try to give voice to people who would be critical of your findings?

• **Use undercover techniques carefully.** At various town meetings, I show a hard-hitting investigative story about a Cincinnati road supervisor who had taken repeated taxpayer-financed trips to Las Vegas to attend trade shows. WCPO-TV, a station well-respected for its outstanding investigative work, used undercover techniques to document how the supervisor and two of his assistants never attended one minute of the convention but spent days at gambling tables and restaurants. Then the station confronted the supervisor and even showed him the undercover tape of him hanging out and placing bets at the casino. After the investigation, the supervisor took early retirement and his two underlings had to pay the county government thousands of dollars in travel expenses.

The journalists in a town meeting in New Orleans loved the story and roared approval. But viewers reacted differently. They began to feel sorry for the road supervisor, they wondered whether the journalist was being "too rough" on him, and some said they wished he had not lost his job over it. An elementary school teacher in one town meeting asked, "Shouldn't you have to get permission from someone before you take pictures of a person without them knowing it?" When I asked who, for example, journalists should ask for permission to go undercover, she said, "Maybe the police." But the same station, WCPO, also has used undercover tactics to expose police brutality.

Clearly the public and journalists see this issue very differently. In the RTNDF survey, seven in ten news directors said journalists should be allowed to use undercover cameras, while just as many members of the public opposed the idea.

The Baltimore focus group took the issue further, saying that undercover tactics should be used only for stories with overwhelming public importance. They said that, most often, TV stations use undercover cameras to target "little guys," not big violators. They said if TV stations are going to use undercover investigation techniques, they should invest more time to be sure that what is shown on TV is part of an ongoing pattern, not just a one-time occurrence.

As you work on a story, ask yourself: Does this story warrant undercover techniques? Are there any other ways of gaining the information? Is the station willing to invest the time and effort to be sure what it discovers undercover is part of a pattern and not a single incident? What motivations does the station have for going under cover? Stations should use undercover investigations only when the technique will uncover important truths that otherwise would go unreported.

• **Develop guidelines for confidential sources.** Without a doubt, confidential sources, like undercover cameras, have helped journalists land stories vital to the public interest. But I stake my flag in the ground to say that reporters use confidential sources too often and that the practice is undermining the public's confidence in what they see on TV (and in every other news medium).

The majority of folks in the Baltimore focus group said journalists use confidential sources too often. "Sometimes they do it to make the story look bigger than it is," one man said. The RTNDF study showed that when confidential sources are used in a story, listeners and viewers believe less of what they see and hear. According to the RTNDF survey, 27 percent of the public said they believed "only a little" of what confidential sources say; 51 percent said they believed only half of what confidential sources say on television. Only 15 percent said they believe "most" of what confidential sources say in television news stories.

Viewers are telling us they cannot weigh the reliability of the information if they don't know the source.

Fifty-nine percent of the general public surveyed said journalists should only be allowed to keep news sources confidential if revealing the source's name would put the person in danger. News directors are much less likely (29 percent) to agree with this idea. In the survey, more than half of viewers (57 percent) said that if a journalist can't get a source to go on the record, then maybe the story should not go on the air. Viewers have told me in public town meetings that they are not even sure the reporters have real sources when they claim to have "confidential sources."

In Baltimore, one woman participating in the town meeting said, "I think the reporters use unnamed sources just to make the story look more important. It makes it look like they have some super secret information."

A man at the same meeting said, "I think the reporters are just talking with each other, trading information, then pretending they have confidential sources."

Tribune Company Publishing president and former editor and publisher of the *Chicago Tribune* Jack Fuller wrote, "The best reason (for using confidential sources) is the one that is most consistent with the basic definition of the journalistic enterprise: In certain circumstances confidentiality can increase the total amount of useful information available to the public. For example, a reporter might, by promising confidentiality, persuade a frightened person to describe a crime he has witnessed. This might lead a newspaper to identify a criminal who otherwise would have gone free."[5]

---

[5]Jack Fuller, *News Values* (Chicago: University of Chicago Press, 1996), 58.

Often, as Fuller says, the identity of the source is one of the most important parts of the story. In fact, Fuller suggests, "The most a reporter should ordinarily promise is that he will not publish the source's name *in the story*, not that he will *never* reveal the name."[6]

As I travel across the country teaching in newsrooms and workshops, I am surprised by how few newsrooms have formal policies or even guidelines about when it is acceptable for a reporter to use an unnamed source in a story.

After the focus group meeting in Baltimore, Bob Steele and I drafted a two-part document to help journalists evaluate the sources they use and then to set the bar high for when and how to use confidential sources:

"WHO SAID THAT?"

Guidelines for Evaluating Sources

- How does this source know this information? How can I confirm the source's information through government records, other documents, further reporting, or other sources?
- Are there underlying assumptions on which my source depends that I should question?
- How representative is my source's point of view? Who else knows what my source knows?
- What is the past reliability and reputation of this source?
- What is the source's motive for providing the information? What does this source have to gain or lose? Will this information make the source look better, worse, guilty, or innocent?
- What is my relationship with the source?
- Why am I using this source? Did I use this source because I am in a rush and this source often gives good quotes and soundbites on deadline? How often do others or I use this source?
- Do I fear losing this source? How does that perception color my judgment? How am I being manipulated by this source?
- Where can I find an independent person who has the expertise on the subject of this story and can help me verify/interpret/ challenge the information my source has given me?

---

[6]Ibid., 60

Guidelines for Interviewing Confidential Sources: Who, When, Why?

Fulfill *all* of the following criteria, then consider the other questions listed below.

- A story that uses confidential sources should be of overwhelming public concern.
- Before using an unnamed source, you must be convinced there is no other way to get the essential information *on the record*.
- The unnamed source must have verifiable and first-hand knowledge of the story. Even if the source cannot be named, the information must be proven true. If you are unsure the information is true, admit it to the public. A promise of confidentiality may protect a liar or a manipulator and the promise may make it difficult or even impossible for the journalist to ever set the record straight.
- You should be willing to reveal to the public why the source cannot be named and what, if any, promises the news organization made in order to get the information.
- Only in the rarest cases of all should a journalist allow a confidential source to assert something damaging to an individual, particularly a private individual. The ban against allowing confidential sources being allowed to attack someone else and remain nameles should be nearly absolute.

Questions to consider:

- What does the use of a confidential source mean to the factual accuracy and contextual authenticity of your story?
- Does this source deserve the protection of his or her identity?
- What legal obligations do you incur by promising not to reveal this source's name? If you are sued, are you willing to go to jail to protect this source? If you are sued, will the source come forward and be named? Is the reluctance justifiable?
- How would viewers evaluate the same information if they knew the source's name and motivations?
- What have you done to help the source understand the risks he or she is taking by giving you information?
- If you promised to protect a source's identity, are you using production techniques that will ensure the protection you promised? What if a lawyer subpoenas the raw tapes? Would

the person be identifiable in the tape outtakes? You should understand your newsroom's policy on confidentiality before you promise it to sources. You may need the consent of an editor and/or you may have to, by policy, reveal a source's identity to a supervisor. Your source should be told you might have to identity him or her to at least one supervisor in your newsroom.

REMEMBER: Seek many truths. Constantly evaluate the sources you use in stories. What motives do your sources have to provide you information? How can you verify the information they give you? Use confidential sources and undercover investigative techniques sparingly and only when they involve issues of overwhelming public significance that cannot be proven true by more overt means.

• **Bidding for news.** Be wary of sources who offer information in exchange for favors or money. Journalists should not pay for interviews. When journalists pay sources for information, it creates a motive for the source to provide information that he or she does not know to be true. The source might be motivated by a paycheck to fabricate information, obtain documents and information illegally, violate confidences, or alter photographs, videotape, or documents.

"Checkbook journalism" also might motivate amateur photographers or stringers to take unwarranted risks in order to capture images they can sell. On the other hand, it should be acceptable for journalists to pay a reasonable "stringer fee" for pictures or videotape of newsworthy events if they can verify the pictures to be true and accurate. When journalists air pictures they have purchased from someone else, that business arrangement should be disclosed to the public.

When I was a news director, a call came into the WSMV newsroom one day that two Blackhawk helicopters had crashed into each other while on a routine training mission at Fort Campbell, sixty miles away. We initially heard "there were multiple fatalities and no survivors." In what I recall to be minutes after the crash, a freelance photographer who had been taking pictures of the mission for families of the soldiers involved called to say he had "very good" video of the crash that he wanted to sell. I told him I wanted the video and we agreed on a price. (I recall the price to be $500.) A few minutes later, he called to say somebody else had offered more. I told him I would pay $1,000 but that I would not go further. We agreed to the price again and agreed on a deal to deliver the tape. The transaction never took place.

Networks launched into a bidding war over the tape and within a couple of hours, CBS had secured the rights to the crash video for what was reported to be more than $20,000. I purchased still pictures of the crash from a freelance photographer who was standing next to the video photographer. The still photographer asked me to make a $1,000 donation to a fund for the dead soldiers' families. I wish I could say why $1,000 seemed ethical to me but $20,000 did not. One price seems to me to be a fee for photographic services; the higher number seems to be profiteering over somebody else's misfortune.

A personal confession: I have to admit that if our network (NBC) had bought the pictures, I am sure we would have run the video, which showed what happened more clearly than anyone could describe.

While trying to decide how much to pay for valuable video, journalists should consider whether the person who shot the video was acting in a journalist's capacity or was a participant in the story. Newsrooms pay journalists; they should not pay for interviews.

Checkbook journalism takes other forms. Some newsrooms hire consultants to be readily available to talk on the record about such issues as defense, aviation safety, and medicine. Those paid consultant relationships should be disclosed to the public, especially when the consultant is a former government employee such as a military general or political strategist for a campaign or administration. Of course, there is the danger that the consultant might be more willing to speculate about matters if the person is afraid that, by not speculating, he or she might lose a paycheck.

• **Make the size of story and promotions fit size of problem.** Plenty of thoughtful newsrooms undermine their good journalism by airing shrieking and overblown story promotions. TV stations should not make promises in promotions they can't deliver on in the newscasts. Promotions should not raise unwarranted fears or exaggerate the importance of a story. Journalists should weigh the amount of promotion their station is giving to a story against the story's real importance. Is this a big problem or an isolated incident? How much space, airtime, or prominent play does this story deserve? The tone of the promotion should match the tone and content of the story. Have you used inflated, subjective language in pre-show headlines, promos, or teases? What kind of music is running beneath promos that could color the viewer's perception of the story?

• **Be honest with viewers.** Is this a four-month investigation or four days of investigations spread over four months? Is the station willing to explain to the public the resources it spent, the tactics, methods, sources, and evidence? Are you willing to admit what you don't know or what you still need to know?

• **Correct reporting mistakes quickly and publicly.** The ASNE survey found that the public is alert to mistakes the media make in coverage. ASNE's study concluded, "Members of the public who have had actual experience with the news process are the most critical of media credibility. The same is true of journalists who have been the subjects of news stories. Americans based a large part of their views of journalism credibility on their personal experience, or that of their acquaintances, in being the subject of news stories, or their personal knowledge of situations reported in the press. Experience with the press is frequently negative.

"Sizeable numbers of both journalists and members of the public say they found errors in articles about themselves or things they know from personal experience. Frequently, it's a matter of misinterpretation, but often a matter of factual mistakes."[7]

The 1998 RTNDF study showed that viewers do not penalize or think less of journalists who correct mistakes. Clearly, admitting mistakes and errors is not only a wise practice, but also a very desirable one among viewers. One caveat: While viewers do appreciate honest and prompt corrections, journalists do not have a license to make the same mistakes over and over.

Newspapers and even some Web sites have corrections policies, but, in my opinion, TV stations are less judicious about correcting mistakes on the air. Think about it. On an almost daily basis newspapers list corrections from previous days' coverage, including spelling and factual errors. But when did you last hear a TV station correcting such errors on the air? Is it that TV journalists don't make those mis-

[7]"Perspectives of the Public and the Press; examining our credibility," The American Society of Newspaper Editors, 1999.

takes, or that TV newsrooms do not have the same values? Stress accuracy. If you make a mistake, admit it, and correct it.

REMEMBER: Be honest. Be honest with your viewers about how you obtained video or information. Be honest in your promotions. Be honest enough to admit when you make mistakes in your stories and correct those mistakes as quickly as possible. The correction should get the same on-air prominence and emphasis as the mistaken information got.

ATTACK DOGS, WATCHDOGS, AND GUIDE DOGS

In that 1999 Baltimore town meeting that I mentioned at the beginning of this chapter, I asked the viewers what they thought about the idea that journalists have a certain "watchdog" function—holding the powerful accountable and giving voice to the voiceless.

The Baltimore residents and those of many other focus groups in New Orleans, Philadelphia, Oklahoma City, Atlanta, and more, have said they are not sure journalists can or do fulfill such a watchdog function. I asked the Baltimore group, "OK, if you don't want journalists to be 'watchdogs,' what kind of dogs do you want them to be?"

One man spoke up. "I want you to be golden retrievers."

I was already sorry I had started down this line of questioning, but I asked him to explain his answer anyway.

"Golden retrievers are versatile," he said. "They can be guide dogs, they can be guard dogs, they sniff out drugs from airport baggage, they are great companions. They are smart, good looking, and don't go around barking at every little noise. I think news people are like those little yap dogs that some people have. They yap at everything, they get up on your furniture, and they pee on everything." By now, the whole room was laughing, except the journalists.

With his dog metaphor, this man, an ordinary viewer put his finger on a central problem. RTNDF's 1998 study found that while 92 percent of news directors think an important function of local TV news is to act as a watchdog looking over local government, only 62 percent of the public agrees. The viewers we met that night in Baltimore were trying to tell us that they believed journalism served an important function but that journalists had given up their role as truth seekers and truth tellers in favor of self-promotion and profiteering.

Viewers believe powerful advertisers, businessmen, and politicians have great influence on news content. How could your coverage confirm or dispel such notions? Does your news reporting, for example, go after the biggest polluters, or just the little garage owner who spills a barrel of oil on the ground? How are the wealthy and powerful people in your community held accountable on your newscasts compared with coverage of the powerless and poor?

Great investigations don't just pick on little guys; the best investigations hold the powerful accountable and give voice to the voiceless. Be vigilant and courageous in seeking and telling truths.

REMEMBER: Be courageous. Hold the powerful accountable and give voice to those who are seldom heard. The overarching principle for journalists is to seek truths and tell them as fully as possible.

ACT INDEPENDENTLY

I think this is the toughest of the guiding principles. Reporters and producers often feel powerless. Bosses tell them what to do, whom to interview, and sometimes even what video to use in their stories. When bosses pressure journalists to "turn stories" that will produce ratings but compromise our principles, how can we be independent? How can a reporter, photojournalist, or producer stand up to a boss who spikes a controversial story about an advertiser or not give favored treatment to a powerful politician when others on the staff do?

An ethical journalist's best defense is to have given detailed thought to his or her principles before the situation arises. Thoughtful journalists can raise questions with bosses that might not have been considered and offer alternatives that go beyond the typical "Do we cover...?" conversations that arise with a heated ethics issue. The thoughtful journalist presses the conversation toward "*How* do we cover this story?".

Journalistic independence begins with accepting personal accountability for our own biases, decisions, and actions. No boss can force you to act unethically. You may choose to follow an order because you don't want to lose your job or you choose not to fight over this particular issue at this time. But those are choices.

CONFLICTS OF INTEREST

Journalists should avoid conflicts of interest, whether the conflicts are real or perceived. It is impossible for any of us to be "objective" in our reporting. For example, I am:

- A gun owner
- Divorced and remarried
- A minivan driver
- A Methodist
- A parent of internationally adopted children
- White
- A registered Democrat
- Male

Does this mean I, as a reporter, should not be allowed to report on issues of gun control, minivan safety, politics, adoption, or issues involving divorce? Of course not. In fact, one might argue that I am more qualified to cover gun issues since I actually own a gun. I might be very good at reporting about minivans since I drive one.

The main test is whether the causes I support profit in some way by my journalism. Imagine the conflicts that arise when a journalist's spouse decides to run for public office, or if a journalist is married to a politically or socially active spouse. For example, before we met, my wife, a psychotherapist, often appeared in the media commenting on issues about relationships, stress, and family. But once we married, we decided it would be inappropriate for her to appear on newscasts at the station where I was the news director. We didn't want reporters to wonder whether they had to treat her with kid gloves in an interview. We didn't want the public to wonder if she was appearing on TV as a way of promoting her family therapy practice.

If journalists have unavoidable conflicts that compromise their independence, they should disclose those conflicts. We can't control and often can't even influence the actions of others. Family members run for political office, make controversial public statements, can be victims of crimes, and can even become criminals. Journalists must do all they can to distance themselves from stories about those people.

The public has a need to know about personal conflicts that compromise a journalist's independence. If an automotive reporter, for example, owned stock in a car company, wouldn't the public want/need to know that while reading a glowing report on the newest model the company just built? Merely disclosing the conflicts does not absolve the journalist, but the disclosure gives viewers a filter through which they can see and sort the information in the story.

Valerie Hyman, founder of the broadcast program at Poynter, put it very well when she said, "Our job as journalists requires us to admit our biases and find ways to report around them." That is part of showing journalistic independence.

The Society of Professional Journalists Code of Ethics says: "Journalists should remain free of associations and activities that may compromise integrity or damage credibility. Journalists should shun secondary employment, political involvement, public office, and service in community organizations if the outside work compromises journalistic integrity."

This point can be a tough one for some journalists. It means resisting the temptation to join groups, foundations, and associations that *are, now or might someday* become newsworthy. The journalist's first obligation is to the (viewing) public. This also means journalists should avoid public displays of support for or against political causes. It means journalists should avoid putting bumper stickers on their cars or signs in their yards favoring or opposing issues that their station is covering or might cover as news stories. This point can become particularly difficult when spouses or family members are involved in high-profile issues or causes.

Station management often encourages or even demands that news anchors "get plugged in" to the community by serving on charitable boards or committees for everything from the United Way to charitable hospitals. While that kind of worthy work can benefit the community and help the journalist gain public stature and visibility, charities often find themselves at the center of pointed news stories, and hospitals could easily find themselves as the target of lawsuits alleging malpractice or financial irregularities. The journalist should remain free to aggressively report on such matters without fear or favor.

Journalists should also avoid taking freelance jobs if the work has the potential to compromise the journalist's independence. For example, a journalist should not cover a story about a factory opening, then write a story for that same company's newsletter. A journalist covering a college or professional sports team should not be paid or employed by the team in any way.

This issue arose in my newsroom when a movie company came to town and wanted journalists to play reporters and anchors in the movies. I was against the idea, but several of my staff wanted to be in the film. I allowed it, but banned them from covering any story about the movie. I think now that I made a mistake, I should not have allowed the journalists in my newsroom to appear in the movie. The public already is confused about the difference between reality and fantasy. The movie business made news in our town a few times. Once a script was stolen from an actress' hotel room. Another time a Teamsters' strike held up production. Journalists shouldn't be actors. They should be the real thing. Journalists have no business being paid by movie companies that might become the focus of news coverage.

A good "sniff test" is to ask, "What would my viewers say if they knew what I was doing?"

I have a few friends in journalism who carry this canon to what I think is an unnecessary extreme. They do not vote in elections because they fear the act of voting will legitimize the public's notion that they are "biased." Of course, they are biased; we all are. Journalists need only to find ways to report around those biases.

Tribune Publishing President Jack Fuller says, "Journalists often end up in close relationships with people who make news. Now that some journalists themselves have become celebrities, and newspapers are covering each other as a beat, even within the cloister it is not possible to avoid such situations. The best approach to the problem of the conflict between friendship and craft combines sensitivity to the reasonable expectations of the person one is dealing with and openness about the conflicting loyalties in play. For example, if an editor is having dinner with a friend in a family setting and the friend tells the editor that he has been nervous lately because the prominent company of which he is an executive is in financial difficulty, the editor might explain at that point that he assumes his friend does not mean for this to be made public and it would make the editor uncomfortable to learn any more about the matter because this is something his newspaper would print if it learned of it under other circumstances."[8]

A journalist's primary loyalty is to the public. Nothing else comes first.

• **Refuse gifts, food, favors, fees, free travel, or special treatment.** When Bob Selwyn hired me as a reporter at WSMV in 1984, he explained the newsroom's guidelines for accepting food and gifts saying, "We have a 'stand and snack' rule. If you can eat or drink it standing up, it is fine. If it is a sit-down dinner, then take a pass."

That common-sense guideline might allow reporters to drink a cup of coffee and down a doughnut, but it would not allow them to eat a prime rib dinner on somebody else's dime. Selwyn also sent out an annual memo near the holiday season reminding journalists not to accept invitations to parties from people who might seek to influence coverage. WSMV reporters and photojournalists understood, for example, that we were not to attend the governor's Christmas party at the mansion. The event was purely social, not a news briefing or newsmaking event. More than once, in fact, our newsroom did news stories about reporters from newspapers, radio, and other TV stations eating lunch on the governor's dime.

If Christmas season cocktails with the governor are off limits, then free tickets to theme parks, circuses, and sporting events are off the charts of unacceptable behavior.

Off-duty journalists should never use their press privileges to gain access to events or areas that any other member of the public does not have access to. For example, off-duty journalists should not use press credentials to watch a football game from the sidelines or go backstage at a concert.

Off duty or on the job, journalists should resist VIP treatment from those who might seek to influence coverage or obtain preferential news coverage in the future. The key question for journalists is *not* whether there *is* a conflict of interest. Journalists should avoid even the *appearance* of a conflict of interest. Business reporters, for example, should not

---

[8]Jack Fuller, *News Values* (Chicago: University of Chicago Press, 1996), 61.

buy or sell stock based on information they gather in the course of their reporting.

• **Disclose unavoidable conflicts.** When MSNBC, for example, reports a story about Microsoft, it routinely discloses that it is partly owned by the computer giant. If a local bank sponsors a specific part of your newscast and now you find yourself reporting about banking irregularities involving that institution, you should disclose the relationship.

Politicians in most states are required by law to disclose potential personal or financial conflicts of interest they might have with legislation that comes before them. Newsrooms should establish similar standards for journalists to disclose potential conflicts to their newsroom supervisors so the decision makers can determine whether another journalist should take over the story.

If a member of your news staff finds himself or herself in legal trouble, the station should ask itself, "If this person was anyone other than a station employee, would it be news?" In fact, a good case can be made for reporting some stories involving journalists that might not be reported otherwise, such as a drunken driving or a domestic violence arrest. The more high profile the journalist, the higher the responsibility of the newsroom to report the story.

Former *St. Petersburg Times* editor Eugene Patterson set a standard for this kind of public disclosure.[9] In July 1976, while editor, he was arrested for driving under the influence of alcohol. According to Bob Haiman, who was the newspaper's managing editor at the time, "Gene has been to a cocktail party at a friend's house. As he was driving home from an American bicentennial party with his wife, he pulled up alongside another car at a stop light, was a bit too close and the cars' doors 'kissed' slightly side to side with almost no visible damage. Cops came, asked Gene if he had anything to drink and he said yes. They gave him the breath test and he came in barely over the limit, by a few thousandths of a point. Although he seemed sober, he failed the test."

Editor Patterson called his newsroom. He ordered Haiman to write a story about the arrest. Haiman protested, "I told him we almost never published stories about simple DWIs, unless there was a big accident, a spectacular crash, injuries, death, high-speed chase, somebody who was falling down drunk at the wheel, and none of these was the case here. But he insisted. So we wrote a four- or five-paragraph story."

---

[9]"Times Editor Arrested," *St. Petersburg Times,* July 6, 1976, sec. A, p. 1.

When Patterson insisted that the story play on the front page, Haiman said, "I *really* protested then, saying the *Times* was a strictly departmentalized paper with national and international news on Page A-1 and the big local stories on page B-1. 'Hell Gene,' I said, 'If it was the city manager we'd probably only put it on 3-B, so why the hell isn't B-1 enough play for Gene Patterson, the editor?'"

Haiman said Patterson replied, "It's precisely because I am the editor, Bob." And Haiman recalls Patterson saying, "As a good and honest newspaper, we are always printing embarrassing news that somebody wishes we wouldn't print—so we can never go easy on ourselves. In fact we have to bend over backward to be tough on ourselves. We should hold ourselves to a notch above the very highest standard we'd ever use to judge anyone else."

The paper published the arrest on in the lower right-hand column of Page A-1. Haiman says the reaction from the community, in letters, phone calls, and talk on the street was overwhelmingly positive and complimentary that the *Times* would report on its own editor's troubles. Patterson says, "Not all of the feedback was positive. For years afterward, when the *Times* would run a liberal editorial, I would get mail from conservatives saying, 'Well I see the editor's drunk again.' All you could do is laugh, which is what they were doing."

Haiman told me, "A few years later, what Gene had sown so well at his own expense, I reaped: A politician who'd been arrested for DWI called me to try to keep the story out of the paper. I said we couldn't do that. He got furious and shouted, 'Well, I bet if it was Gene Patterson you God-damn well would not print it!' I smiled and said, 'As a matter of fact, commissioner, we would, and did; and put it on page A-1. So you have no cause at all to object to the story about you being in the B Section, do you?'"

Reporting such stories says to the viewer that you hold your own profession to the same high standards to which you hold others. Of course, just reporting the story does not erase the damage that journalists cause when they commit an illegal or immoral act. But when stations report their own dirty laundry, it can be a signal to the public that the station's coverage knows no sacred cows.

We also should be willing to expose the unethical practices of other journalists. We hold others to a high standard; and we should expect no less of our own craft. When journalists show that they are capable and willing to self-regulate their profession, it presents a stronger defense against those on the outside who would seek to curb press freedoms.

JOURNALISM AND BUSINESS VALUES

There is no doubt that local television journalists are feeling the pressure to produce more news for less money, while advertisers are increasingly applying more pressure to be allowed to dictate or at least influence news content. The Project for Excellence in Journalism, a Washington-based think tank, surveyed 188 news directors in 2001 and found that 47 percent said they have felt pressure from advertisers to provide positive coverage of their businesses. Almost one out of five news directors (18 percent) said an advertiser had tried to kill a story or prevent negative coverage; about half of all stations surveyed said they include advertising logos on the screen during newscasts. In smaller markets (those with fewer than 376,000 households), the pressure to bow to advertisers is even more intense. Two-thirds of news directors in the smallest markets say they feel pressure to provide positive coverage to sponsors.[10]

The study found that car dealerships and restaurants were particularly interested in stopping negative stories. Some news directors say they no longer go after stories about car dealers; one said a car dealer was successful in killing a story the newsroom wanted to air. Two stations said restaurants had the power to kill negative stories. The report quoted news directors as saying, "The pressure to do puff pieces about sponsors occurs 'constantly,' 'all the time,' 'everyday,' 'routinely,' and 'every time a sales person opened his/her mouth.'" Another news manager said, "It is getting harder every year to maintain the wall between sales and news."

The public has detected this trend of advertisers pressuring television news coverage for some time. Almost all the Baltimore participants said they believe that people who buy commercials on a TV or radio station get more favorable coverage than those who don't. In a half-dozen town meetings in a half-dozen cities around the country in 2000 and 2001, I asked the question, "If a car dealer in this town bought a quarter of a million dollars' worth of ads at a TV station, do you think the car dealer could expect some positive news coverage of their dealership?" The overwhelming majority of residents said yes. They usually said it should not be that way, but they suspect that, in reality, it is.

The 1998 RTNDF survey heard the same thing. The survey asked news directors and the public:

---

[10]"Local TV news project 2001: Gambling With the Future," November 16, 2001, *www. journalism.org,* Washington, D.C.

"How often is news reporting improperly influenced by advertisers?"

News Directors

Often	10 percent
Sometimes	33 percent
Rarely	36 percent

The Public

Often	51 percent
Sometimes	33 percent
Rarely	9 percent

Eighty-four percent, more than eight out of ten Americans questioned, say advertisers can influence news content. Only half as many news directors said advertisers had that power.

Now, more journalists are starting to admit they are feeling the pressure. Reporters, producers, and photojournalists sometimes feel powerless in this struggle. But even non-managers can be powerful and influential when they raise thoughtful questions about the newsroom's position on the separation of business and journalism. Newsrooms should consider writing their own "standards and practices" for thinking about the appropriate wall between news and sales. I recommend you write such guidelines before you're in the middle of a heated battle about a particular story or issue. Front-end conversations are always more effective than back-end conversations held under the heat of deadlines or when angry clients are pounding on the general manager's door.

Guidelines should recognize that advertisers and sponsors are not villains and that journalists need not become "Davids" out to slay advertising "Goliaths" just to prove their journalistic independence.

Bob Steele and I drafted these guidelines for balancing the sometimes competing pressures of journalism and business:

- Do not let the pressure for profits undermine your obligation to produce high quality, ethically sound journalism. **News coverage should not be for sale.**
- Build and sustain a high degree of communication and trust among station leadership and staff members in all departments.
- Don't show favoritism to advertisers. Don't punish businesses just because they do advertise as a way of exercising your editorial independence.
- Don't generate news content just to provide a vehicle for advertising.

- Journalists are in the business of telling news, not selling products.
- A journalist's most important public service is to report the news; everything else comes second.
- Avoid real or perceived conflicts that arise when commercialism underwrites journalism.
- Don't allow commercialism to buy a higher profile in your reporting than is journalistically justified. Use caution in covering sponsored events.
- Don't run promotional material that viewers/listeners could confuse with news.
- Avoid "tie-in" stories to prime time, entertainment programming that has no journalistic value. Do not allow your news judgment to be skewed by the pressures to hold or attract audiences.
- Journalists should remain independent of the business associations that stations legitimately have with advertisers.
- Don't trade on the good name of your organization by accepting favors or gifts not available to the general public.
- Make sure your online product is consistent with the high journalistic and ethical standards of your on-air product.

REMEMBER: Journalists must remain independent. Journalists should find ways to report around their own biases and avoid conflicts of interests or even the appearance of conflicts of interests with those they or their newsroom cover. Where unavoidable conflicts arise, they should be disclosed to the public. Journalists should refuse gifts, favors, and special treatment from those who might be the subject of news coverage or who might seek to influence news coverage. Journalists should respect the business side of their business while not allowing news content to be sold or compromised.

Minimize Harm

Take special notice that this guideline is third on Steele's guiding principles list, not first. It is that way for a reason. If we *start* our decision making by asking, "How can we cause the least harm?" we won't report many important stories.

Journalism is a messy business. Sometimes journalists invade privacy, take pictures of people who don't want to be photographed, and ask probing questions of people who don't want to talk or be held accountable. The job of a journalist is to seek truths. However, as the SPJ Code of Ethics puts it, "Pursuit of the news is not a license for arrogance."

Journalists should be aggressive and show respect. As Steele says, "The journalist's guideline should not be 'never invade privacy'; it should be to 'respect privacy.'"

Many professions require their practitioners to ask pressing questions. When I visited my doctor last year for my annual physical, I was a little bit surprised when she asked me, "Do you need to take an AIDS test this year?" I told her I was surprised at the question and she responded, "Al, I'm your doctor; I am supposed to ask good questions." Our professions have similar demands. We both are to ask tough and detailed questions. But journalists, like doctors, should only invade privacy when they can justify their actions.

Trish Van Pilsum started as a reporter at WCCO-TV in Minneapolis and covered the police beat for many years. "They used to call me Trish and Tragedy," she once told a Poynter class while talking about her early years in reporting on the "death and destruction beat." She said she would sometimes approach tragic stories knowing that, "I can't make the situation any better by reporting on it, but I can do my best not to make it any worse." It is no wonder Trish often landed interviews with vulnerable people who would not speak with other journalists.

Recognize that private people have a greater right to control information about themselves than do public officials and others who seek power, influence, or attention. Only an overriding public need can justify intrusion into anyone's privacy.

The RTNDF study found that, "Almost half (48 percent) of the ·ılts surveyed say local TV news goes too far in disclosing public fig-
' private lives; only 11 percent of news directors agree. Eight per-

cent of adults say the media don't go far enough in exploring the private lives of public figures; thirteen percent of news directors agree."

But when, if ever, should journalists report about the private information about private people? Sometimes people by fate or circumstances become publicly known even if they want to stay out of the limelight. Consider, for example, how you would handle information that a winner of a multi-million dollar lottery had a criminal background. The crimes were years ago. What if that same person's crimes were all financial crimes in which he bilked small investors out of millions of dollars?

At issue is how the lottery win relates to the criminal past. Clearly if the lottery winner chooses to hold news conferences and to portray himself as a philanthropic angel, the journalist has more license and maybe even more of an obligation to set the record straight. How would your decisions change if the financial crimes involved a few thousand dollars? What if he had repaid all of the victims twenty years ago?

Journalists should usually give crime victims more privacy than they give to criminals. Crime victims usually are caught in the vortex of a news story by circumstance and bad luck. Trish's "try to cause no further harm" guideline is a good one. But that does not mean that crime victims should always be shielded from the public. While journalists do not name every victim of spousal abuse, they might if the victim is the mayor or the police chief's spouse.

• **Do not shoot now and ask questions later.** Journalists can cause harm just by asking questions, taking pictures, or obtaining information, even if they do not air what they record or find. Think how you would feel if someone started asking questions of your family and friends about your past, your finances, or your business.

Steele says journalists should ask, "How can I better understand this person's vulnerability and desire for privacy? Can I make a better decision by talking with this person? What alternative approaches can I take in my reporting and my storytelling to minimize the harm of privacy invasion while still fulfilling my journalistic duty to inform the public? For instance, can I leave out some 'private' matters while still accurately and fairly reporting the story? Or can I focus more on a system failure issue rather than reporting intensely on one individual?"

• **Show good taste. Avoid pandering to lurid curiosity.** A second-grade teacher in the Baltimore focus group said she used to tell her students to watch the evening news and report back to the class what they learned can't do that anymore," she said, noting that violence and graphic images pervade newscasts and make them too disturbing for her students.

I asked the focus group to watch two different television stations' stories from the same night. The stories were about a man who had climbed to the top of a radio tower. After several hours on the tower, the man fell to his death in full view of a gathered crowd.

Focus group members said they were disturbed by how the local newscasts "got so excited about the story." They wondered whether the story should have any place in a newscast. The group did not seem to be telling journalists to never show violent images. They said we broadcast those images when, too often, they are not really news.

Graphic images of violence may be newsworthy and should not be ruled out just because they are disturbing. Ask, "What do the viewers need to see and when do they need to see them?" How would you justify the use of graphic images to the public and to your newsroom?

The RTNDF national study asked if reporters are insensitive to people's pain when they report on victims of accidents or crime. Thirty-four percent of the general public said it was a major problem. Only 15 percent of news directors say insensitivity is a "major problem."

On April 21, 1994 a middle school student was shot and killed in Nashville, Tennessee. The teacher was treating the class to a movie, *Beauty and the Beast*. It was to have been a light and fun afternoon for the kids. But one young boy carried a gun to school that day. In the darkened classroom, the gun fired, and another middle school student was killed.

We responded to the shooting with wall-to-wall live coverage. One of WSMV's best spot news photojournalists, Toney Cook, arrived on the scene quickly, as he often did in breaking news situations. He walked beside paramedics as they wheeled the young shooting victim on a gurney toward a waiting ambulance. One paramedic pumped the injured boy's chest. We were jarred by the image when Toney microwaved the tape back to the station. Toney told me he felt fairly certain the boy would die before he made it to the hospital.

My first instinct was not to run this graphic video. Not ever. After a few minutes, I decided to call some people I trusted on such matters. One of them was Nashville child psychologist Warren Thompson, who had served as an adviser to the city schools on issues of violence. I described the scene to Warren and asked him what arguments he would ke in favor of running the pictures. I intentionally framed the ques- that way because I knew all of the reasons I might not run the video. I needed to know whether there were reasons I might consider running pictures of a young boy dying on an EMT's gurney.

Thompson surprised me when he said, "Oh yes, I think you should run it." He said he thought it was important for young people and for their community to see that guns in school hurt people. He explained that young people see a lot of violence, but usually it is "happy violence," like Rambo killing the bad guys or Bruce Willis enduring all manner of shooting and fighting and, just before the closing credits roll, escaping the bad guys and establishing justice.

Thompson recommended I adopt a few guidelines for using the video. He said he would not run the pictures in headlines or teases; he would not use the video over and over, just that day. And he said, "You need to warn the viewers that they are going to see some pretty disturbing stuff." It was excellent advice. We invited Thompson to be with us on the set that night to explain how parents should talk with their kids about the images they were seeing on the news that night.

The shooting at John Trotwood Moore Middle School became a far more significant event than we anticipated. Over the next few years, our newsroom would respond to more shootings inside schools. November 15, 1995 a student killed a teacher and fellow student and wounded another teacher at Richland High School, Lynnville, Tennessee. December 1, 1997, a student opened fire at Heath High School near Paducah, Kentucky. The fourteen-year-old boy killed three students and wounded seven others. May 19, 1998, our news crews were on the scene of a fourth school shooting in four years. Two days before his graduation, an honor student opened fire in a parking lot of the Lincoln County High School in Fayetteville, Tennessee. The next year, the nation gasped at the unspeakable horrors that unfolded at Columbine High School in Colorado.

The lessons from the 1994 shooting guided how we covered the others. Looking back, I see that we used the same principles Steele recommends:

- **Seek truth and tell it as fully as possible.** Find ways to show the pictures so the viewers can fully understand what happened and how this can be prevented in the future.
- **Act independently.** We tried to be independent of the pressures we felt for ratings and public approval and to recognize our own biases about the images. Several of us i[n] newsroom were parents of young children. I had a middl[e]

school-aged child at the time. I believe that one of my gut reactions was to want to protect kids like her from the graphic images we intended to show on TV. In the end, showing those images may have been a caring act.

- **Minimize harm.** Forewarn the viewers about what they are going to see, and explain why we chose to use the images. Sometimes TV stations call these "disclaimers." I wish we would call them "claimers" in which we would claim responsibility for our decision to show the video. We also limited the tone of our writing and the number of times we showed the images.

9-1-1 CALLS

Making tough calls on deadline is a skill that gets easier with practice. On an almost daily basis, working journalists call my colleagues at The Poynter Institute and me to ask questions about how they might handle a tough ethics decision. One question I have encountered over and over as a journalist and now as a teacher is how and when to use audio recordings of 9-1-1 calls. Sometimes the recordings, albeit disturbing to the viewer, can be valuable if the journalist is trying to show that the dispatcher did not follow protocols in dispatching help or giving advice to help a victim. Miami television stations had to make a decision about whether to air a 9-1-1 call a few minutes before their 5 P.M. newscast. The caller was a desperate woman who had driven her car into a Dade County canal. The woman was confused and did not know her exact location. She drowned while talking on the phone to the dispatcher. Two network affiliated stations did not air the tape. One read a transcript of the tape. Another station played the tape up to the moment of death. In the days that followed, it became clear that the dispatcher had not given appropriate instructions to the victim to open a window and try to escape. The tape became vitally important information for the public to hear in order to understand what went wrong.

It is my experience, watching news stories from around America over the years, that journalists most often use 9-1-1 recordings to ratchet the emotions of the story, not to expose any system failure or other important journalistic truth. When journalists air 9-1-1 recordings they re-victimize the victim or their family while not serving the pub- recordings might also cause great embarrassment to the caller if the person uses graphic language or shows fear or confusion, which are all normal responses to extreme stress. Before using such tapes, journalists should warn the victim's family that the tape is going to be on TV. It is not the same as asking permission, but it is a fair warning.

STRONG PICTURES — WEAK CONTENT

Sometimes television stations decide to air stories not because they affect many people but just because the story contains "great pictures." Sacramento TV stations were confronted with such a case June 9, 2000, when a Sacramento high school senior stripped naked on the stage of her class' graduation. As you might imagine, many people with home movie cameras captured the event. The girl jumped off the stage and ran the length of the football field where the ceremony was being held. TV stations had to decide what, if anything, to show. One station aired the video with a mosaic tile effect over the girl's body a total of nine times in two stories over two days. The image popped up over and over. The school system brought public indecency charges against the girl. But stations cannot use that little scap of news to justify using the video so many times, other than the lurid attraction of the pictures. A year later, when school officials issued strong warnings to students not to repeat the stunt, stations and Web sites again trotted out the pictures of the student streaking.

DIRTY WORDS

I sometimes am surprised that newsrooms allow so many graphic images of death and violence to appear on their news but they take a puritanical stand against airing profanity or off-color language. Such salty language is fair and ethical at times. Not airing the off-color words may take away from the authenticity of the story and might even reflect the personal tastes and biases of the journalist.

The raciest language I ever aired was included in a story about a prison boot camp for youthful offenders. The guards at this Georgi boot camp swore at the young inmates from the moment the priso ers awoke to long after lights out. The foul language was part of total treatment. The six weeks of insults, highly regimented s ules, and backbreaking work, in theory, was designed to te inmates the values of self-discipline and self-reliance. We w

viewers that this was not a story about church; it was a story about
prison. We suggested the parents call the kids into the living room,
sit down and watch this story with them, and then talk about it in
depth. Then we warned them again that they were going to hear some
language they would not like, but our hope was that if they saw prison
life on TV it might help them never to see it in person. We did not
get a single complaint call; we got many requests for dubs from Sunday schools, civic groups, and Scout troops.

To bleep or not to bleep. That was the question facing KARE11-
TV, Minneapolis, news director Tom Lindner before the station aired its
"Extra" segment on the 10 P.M. news November 14, 2001.

The story documented the reunion of two long-separated brothers,
Tom and Dean Weisser. As the camera captured the pair's first embrace
in more than two decades, an overcome-by-emotion Dean sobbed to his
wayward brother, "I'll say this again: You could have called, asshole."

The station aired the soundbite uncut and without a bleep. Lindner
said, "It's not normal for us to include language like that in the newscast.
But we thought in the context of the story it made sense. Guys say
things like that to each other. It was a natural moment."[11]

Lindner offers a good test for such circumstances. "How does the
graphic language add to the viewer's understanding? What is your journalistic mission in using the language?" Why do you viewers need to
hear the soundbite "as is?" How would you explain why you used the
soundbite to your viewers? How can you minimize the harm in this case,
including limiting the number of times you use the graphic language
in headlines, teases, or promos. How will you warn the viewers about
the graphic language before it airs?

The most difficult time to make decisions about when to use graphic
or violent images or language is when you are on deadline. Think "front-
end" what your newsroom standards should be. Poynter's Bob Steele says
journalists should ask questions such as:

- What does the public need to know and when does the public
  need to know it?
- Who are the stakeholders involved in this story?
- What would I want to happen if the roles were reversed and I
  was the subject of the story?

Drops the A-Bomb," Mike Mosedale, City Pages Media Inc., Minneapolis, November
age 9.

- How does using this graphic video and/or off-color language serve my journalistic purpose?
- Who have you consulted who could give you solid thinking about this decision?

REMEMBER: **Newsrooms should establish protocols for protecting privacy and airing graphic video and language. Newsrooms should carefully consider the tone and degree of their coverage when the story involves 9-1-1 calls, which often capture people living out the most stressful moments of their lives. The journalist should be able to explain to the public why the graphic language, video, or 9-1-1 call is important to the public's understanding of an important issue or event.**

ETHICS IN CRIME COVERAGE

Even when the suspect is an adult, journalists must make tough calls about when and how to name criminal suspects if the suspect has not been formally charged. Eighty-nine percent of the public that RTNDF questioned in its survey said local news stations should wait until a suspect is charged before naming the person. Seventy percent of news directors in the survey agreed that stations should wait for formal charges before releasing a suspect's name. Before naming suspects who have not been charged, ask yourself:

- How likely is it that the charges will "stick"?
- What is the strength of the evidence?
- What is missing from the evidence and how likely are police to gather those missing parts?
- Who might be harmed if you name the suspect?
- Who might be harmed if you do not name the suspect? somebody else be implicated?

IDENTIFYING JUVENILES

Newsrooms must make tough decisions about when and how to identify juveniles involved in news stories. Gut decisions to identify juveniles can cause unjustified harm. Strict policies against identifying juveniles can prevent the public from understanding important issues.

Yet juveniles deserve a special level of privacy protection, especially those in their pre-teen years, because of their vulnerability.

Journalists can find ways to tell stories involving juveniles that go beyond the daily news event to gather a deeper understanding of the context of a story. But they need to ask themselves some questions before deciding how to go about it. Before deciding whether to identify a juvenile, journalists should consider:

• **Identification:** Who is served by identifying this juvenile? Why does the public need to know the identity? What is the journalistic purpose in identifying the juvenile?

• **Charge:** If the juvenile is charged with a crime, how strong is the evidence? Have formal charges been filed? Is the juvenile only a suspect? How likely are the charges to stick and the juvenile to be prosecuted? If the juvenile is charged with a crime, will the juvenile be tried as an adult?

• **Harm:** What is the severity of the crime, the nature of the crime, how much harm was done in the process of the crime?

• **Implication:** If you do not name the juvenile, who else could be implicated by rumor or confusion about who is charged?

• **Record:** What is this juvenile's record? What is his or her history? How would shielding that juvenile's identification and history expose the public to potential harm? What if you don't name the juvenile? What harm could occur?

• **Exposure:** What is the level of public knowledge? Is the juvenile's identification widely known already? How public was the juvenile's arrest, apprehension, or the incident that landed the juvenile in the public eye?

• **Family:** How does the juvenile's family feel about identifying the g person? Has the family granted interviews or provided informa-
the media? Has the juvenile talked publicly?

• **Damage:** Once a juvenile is identified, some damage is done to that person that can never be completely reversed. If charges against the juvenile are dropped or proven untrue, you may prevent further damage by no longer identifying the juvenile. The journalist should continuously evaluate the decision to name a juvenile, always testing the value of the information against the harm caused to the juvenile.

• **Depth:** How does naming the juvenile allow the journalist to take the story into a deeper, more contextual level of reporting? What would identifying the juvenile allow the journalist to tell a viewer that the audience could not understand otherwise? Perhaps a deeper understanding of the juvenile allows us to understand the circumstances of a crime or incident.

• **Tone:** What is the tone and degree of your coverage? How often would the juvenile be identified? How prominent and in-depth is the coverage? How will the juvenile be characterized in the coverage? What guidelines do you have about the use of the juvenile's picture or name in follow-up stories or continuing coverage?

• **Timing:** When would the identification occur? Minutes, hours, days, or even years after an incident, identification would have different impacts on the juvenile.

• **Legality:** What are the legal implications of your decisions? What laws apply about juvenile identification? What is the position of the presiding court?

• **Understanding:** How old is this juvenile? What is he/she capable of understanding about the situation he/she is involved in?

• **Impact:** Who, besides the juvenile, will be affected by your decision? Other juveniles? Parents? Families? Victims? Officials? Investigators? Courts?

• **Advocate:** In the absence of a parent or guardian, can the journalist find someone who can act in an unofficial capacity to raise concerns on the juvenile's behalf so the juvenile's interests do not get lost in the journalist's quest to tell a story?

• **Alternatives:** What alternatives have you considered to identifying the juvenile?

• **Justification:** How will you explain your decision to identify this juvenile to the public, to your newsroom?

REMEMBER: Newsrooms should establish guidelines for covering stories involving suspects who have not been charged. Juveniles deserve special protection from the public's glare. Newsrooms should not enact a universal ban on naming juveniles however, because sometimes the public has a legitimate need to know as much as possible about a juvenile who is charged with a serious crime.

COVERING STORIES THAT ARE "OFF LIMITS"

Many newsrooms have rules, or at least strong guidelines, against covering stories about bomb threats and suicides. They usually say they do not want to encourage others to become copycats in order to get publicity.

That is, in my opinion, a good-hearted, but wrong-minded way of thinking. Expert journalists find ways to cover these stories, telling as much truth as possible while minimizing the harm they could cause along the way.

Like so many other tough calls we have discussed in this chapter, an hour before a newscast is the worst time to try to make a decision about how to treat such topics as suicides or bomb threats. Conversations grow tense, voices get lost, and emotions rise just before airtime. Have discussions in your newsroom now about how you will cover these stories. How will you handle threatening calls if they should come to your newsroom? Post your guidelines near every telephone; be sure your switchboard has protocols in case the station receives threatening calls. Be prepared. Front-end decisions are the best decisions.

COVERING SUICIDES

According to the American Association of Suicideology, in the United States someone commits suicide every seventeen minutes. It happens eighty-four times a day, more than 30,000 people a year. Yet suicide is one of the most under-reported stories of our time. Suicide is the eighth leading cause of death in the United States. Homicide ranks thirteenth, but homicide receives astronomically more news coverage. There are twenty-five suicide attempts for every one that is completed. At least five million living Americans have attempted suicide.

I first became aware of the need for more suicide coverage when a volunteer for the Nashville Suicide Prevention hotline asked if she could come to our newsroom's morning meeting and talk just for a few minutes about the need for more coverage. That was the first time I had heard that more people kill themselves in most American cities than die of homicide. It was also the first time I had heard a mental health professional suggest that coverage, in the right way, could be valuable in lowering the suicide rate.

One reason suicides are so under-reported in mainstream journalism is linked to an historic newsroom avoidance of covering the topic. By avoiding the story in an effort to minimize potential harm to the victims' families or concern that news coverage might prompt others to take their lives, journalists avoid an important issue that viewers need to understand. Journalists should inform themselves about this important topic so they can cover the story with a high degree of skill, compassion, and knowledge.

Questions for the Newsroom

- What policies or rules does your newsroom have that could trap you from covering the issue of suicides?
- What guidelines do you have about when or how you cover this story? What tone would the coverage take? Where should suicide stories play in a newscast? How much coverage is warranted?
- What exactly are your concerns about covering this topic: the privacy of the individual, the potential harm coverage could cause a grieving family, the public's need to know, the extent to which the death was carried out in public view.
- How well known was the victim or the victim's family? Can we determine the motivations for the death? Were others directly harmed in the act of the suicide? Did others assist in the death? How did the person die and how often does this happen?
- What is the potential harm that could come from not reporting the story? For example, if a teenager kills hims other young people are likely to hear about the death. P

parents might not know about the death of the young person
without media coverage. Parents would not know that they
should be especially alert to changes in the behavior of their
children, who might be in shock. News coverage can alert
parents to be open with their kids about this sensitive topic.

- What guidelines does your newsroom have about how to
  minimize the danger that a story about suicides, especially
  the suicide of a juvenile, could trigger copycat deaths? How
  could your newsroom include, as a matter of policy, the
  phone number of a local crisis line any time you do a suicide
  story?

- How well does the newsroom understand the underlying
  warning signs and motivations of suicide? What experts does
  your newsroom have contact with who can advise the
  newsroom on deadline about how to handle suicide stories.

Here are some guidelines and warning signs published by the American Association of Suicidology.

- In order to discourage copycat suicides, avoid or minimize
  reporting specific details of the method the victim used in
  taking his or her life. Avoid descriptions of a suicide as
  "unexplainable," such as "he had everything going for him."
  Avoid reporting romanticized versions of the reasons for the
  suicide, such as "they wanted to be together for all eternity."
  And avoid reporting simplistic reasons for suicides such as "the
  boy committed suicide because he had to wear braces on his
  teeth." The rationale for suicidal thoughts is much deeper.

- Consider how you play the story. Consider minimizing harm
  by not playing the story in headlines. Consider not using the
  photo of the person. It will make the suicide less glamorous to
  someone who might consider imitating the act.

- Report suicide in a straightforward manner so suicide does not
  appear to be exciting. Reports should not make the suicidal
  person appear admirable nor should they seem to approve of
  suicide.

- Present alternatives to suicide such as calling a suicide hotline
  or getting counseling.
  Whenever possible, present examples of positive outcomes of
  people in suicidal crisis.

Consider educating your audience about how to spot suicide warning signs. A person might be suicidal if he or she:

- Talks about committing suicide
- Has trouble eating or sleeping
- Experiences drastic changes in behavior
- Withdraws from friends and/or social activities
- Loses interest in hobbies, work, school, etc.
- Prepares for death by making out a will and final arrangements
- Gives away prized possessions
- Has attempted suicide before
- Takes unnecessary risks
- Has had recent severe losses
- Is preoccupied with death and dying
- Loses interest in their personal appearance
- Increases his or her use of alcohol or drugs

BOMB THREATS, ANTHRAX THREATS, AND OTHER TOUGH CALLS

There was no doubt in my mind that in the days after the attacks on the World Trade Center and the Pentagon that newsrooms nationwide would see a spike in bomb threats and, as we found out later, in hoaxes involving anthrax. This is an unfortunate by-product of modern terrorist acts. We have seen this sort of thing before. After the school shootings at Columbine High School in Littleton, Colorado, bomb threats closed or disrupted hundreds of schools nationwide.

Well-intentioned journalists often fall on old newsroom rules not to cover bomb threats. The theory is that coverage will only spawn more threats and that the media should not "feed" the panic.

But journalists are in the business of telling the news, not withholding it. Journalists should use a thoughtful tone while covering such stories. The stories should focus more on the underlying issues than on the threatening calls themselves.

Before covering bomb threats or other threats to public safety, answer the following questions:

- What do you know? What do you need to know?
- What do your viewers want to know? What do they need to kno

- What is the real threat to life or property?
- What are the consequences of the event? Reporting a false threat could lead to copycat threats. On the other hand, reporting arrests might discourage such threats. Other consequences might include raising the public's level of insecurity when it is not warranted. Repeated broadcasting of bomb/anthrax hoaxes can have the effect of "crying wolf," and the public becomes less responsive when actual danger arises. But reporting on the volume and range of threats could inform viewers about the pressures under which police and school officials labor. It could be important for the public to understand why officials react as they do.
- How significant is the evacuation and the interruption of normal life in your community?
- What effect does this event have on law enforcement or emergency crews' ability to respond to other calls?
- What else is the story about? What is the story behind the story? What thought are you giving to the bigger issues involved in this story? How easy is it for schools, the phone company, or the police to track down a threatening caller? How seriously are violators treated? Have you ever followed one of these cases through the legal system to find out what happens? How many such bomb/biological threats did the police handle last year? How many resulted in prosecution? How many of those prosecuted went to jail or were actually punished? What was the extent of the punishment? Do your schools have caller ID systems in place? Do they or should they record incoming phone calls?
- Who could help you understand the short-term and long-term consequences of your coverage? Keep a full Rolodex of experts and wise people who can help educate you about the stories you cover. These experts might never be named in your coverage, but they can inform your thinking and reporting.
- How do you explain your decision to your staff and your viewers? How could you justify your decisions about where and how you play stories about bomb/anthrax threats? How much discussion have you had in your newsroom about your coverage?
- Encourage others to be the voice of the contrarian in your decision-making conversations. Who could you turn to who

might offer different perspectives and diverse ideas, in the decision-making process?

- What alternatives can you consider to maximize your truthtelling but minimize the sensationalism of your coverage including: not going live, playing the story deeper in the newscast, and/or not teasing the story in pre-show opens or promotions? How can you justify the positioning of your coverage?

If police evacuate a restaurant because of some suspicious white powder they find on a table, and the powder turns out to be Equal, it was not an anthrax scare. It was an "artificial sweetener scare."

Avoid words such as "chaos," "terror," and "mayhem." They are subjective words. Play it straight, especially at a time when your community or, depending on the gravity of the story, even the nation is tense. Tone down your teases, leads, and graphics. The tone of what you report should not contradict the careful reporting of facts.

Think carefully before going live in covering these stories. You have less editorial control in live situations. The emphasis on live coverage may deflect the attention these stories deserve.

REMEMBER: More people die of suicide than homicide each year in America. It is an important issue that deserves sensitive coverage. A universal ban on covering bomb threats may rob the public of important information about what is going on in their community.

THE DRIVE TO "GO LIVE"

There is no doubt that a journalist can serve a vital public need by reporting live from the scene from some stories. The September 1 2001 attacks on the World Trade Center and the Pentagon were of v public importance, and live reporting allowed viewers worldwi quickly understand the scope and nature of the threat, even as the story was still unfolding. But when journalists report news live, the stories bypass their usual filtering process to test accuracy, tone, and quality. Journalists who produce or report stories live should use special care, sharp skills, and plenty of forethought.

The news director of KCNC-TV, Denver, Angie Kucharski, says, "A good guideline to follow when you are deciding whether to go live is to 'overreact in the newsroom and underreact on the air.'"

QUESTIONS BEFORE YOU GO LIVE

- Beyond competitive factors, what are your motivations for going live? Why do your viewers need to know about this story before journalists have the opportunity to edit, question, or filter the information off the air? What truth testing are you willing to give up in order to speed information to the viewer?

- Are you prepared to air the *worst possible* outcome that could result from this unfolding story (such as a person killing himself or someone else live on TV)? What outcomes are you not willing to air? Why? How do you know the worst possible outcome will *not* occur?

- How does the journalist know that the information he or she has is true? How many sources have confirmed the information? How does the source know what he or she says to be true? What is this source's past reliability? How willing is the source to be quoted?

- What are the short-term and long-term consequences of going on the air with the information? What are the consequences of waiting for additional confirmation or for a regular newscast?

- When you are covering a standoff between a suspect and police live, always assume that the hostage taker, gunman, or terrorist has access to the reporting. Avoid describing or showing any information that could divulge the tactics or positions of SWAT team members or other emergency workers. Be willing to tell viewers why you are withholding certain information if the reasons involve security. Weigh the benefits of reporting the story live to the public compared with the potential harm reporting might cause.

- Newsrooms should have a general prohibition against calling a gunman or a hostage taker. It is difficult to imagine the circumstances under which a newsroom might ethically and responsibly decide to violate this guideline. Journalists are rarely trained in professional hostage negotiations and one wrong question or inappropriate word could jeopardize someone's life. Further, just calling the hostage-taker could tie up phone lines or otherwise complicate negotiators' efforts to communicate with the criminal. When hostage-takers or people making other threats call the newsroom, journalists should notify authorities immediately and resist the temptation to put the caller on the air live.

- Things can go wrong very quickly in a live report, endangering lives or damaging negotiations. Do not report without verifying information you hear on police scanners. Be aware that during live coverage, repeating such information could compromise police negotiations or tactics. Be very cautious in any reporting on the medical condition of hostages until after a crisis is concluded. If a hostage-taker hears on TV that someone he or she may have harmed has died, it could create a new air of desperation. Be cautious about interviewing hostages or released hostages while a crisis continues. There will be time to air such statements once the situation is resolved.

- What is the tone of the coverage? How can the journalist raise viewer awareness while minimizing hype and fear? Who in your newsroom is responsible for monitoring the tone of what is being broadcast?

- What electronic safety net has your station considered to minimize harm, such as a tape and signal delay, that could give you time to dump out of live coverage if the situation turns graphic, violent, or compromises the safety of others?

- How clearly does the technical crew at your TV station understand the newsroom's standard for graphic content? How well are guidelines understood by directors, tape editors, live shot technicians, photojournalists, pilots, or engineers who might have to make an editorial call when the news director o other people in positions of formal authority are not availabl

- What factor does the time of day play in your decision to c a breaking event? If the event occurs when children norm are watching television, how does that fact alter the tone and degree of your coverage?

REMEMBER: Live coverage is an important tool for informing the public but carries with it a great responsibility for journalists to show restraint and professionalism.

Bob Steele often begins his ethics teaching with the statement, "A journalist's most important ethical obligation is to strive for excellence." We expect excellence of doctors, nurses, and police in emergencies; we should expect no less of journalists. Journalists must continuously educate themselves about issues and events in order to report stories in context and educate viewers. Journalists have a moral obligation, an implied contract with the public, to perform with excellence.

Chapter 9

Quick, Get Me Some Disaster Pictures

"A good journalist is a rewarding sight. He must have a zest for events. He must have a dedication to facts and a scent of humbug. He must cultivate skepticism while avoiding cynicism. He must learn to cover causes for which he can have sympathy but must not display loyalty. He must be incorruptible. He must go where he is not wanted, and be resistant to those who are too welcoming. And for all of this, his hours will be long, his pay inadequate, and his standing in the community not particularly high."

THOMAS GRIFFITH, EDITOR OF *LIFE* MAGAZINE

IN TIMES OF SPOT NEWS there is an invisible line that separates informing the public and scaring them. After the attacks on the World Trade Center and the Pentagon, newsrooms had to decide when to stop showing the airplanes drilling into the sides of the buildings. Some newscasts aired the crashing plane pictures five days after the attacks. They ran the video frame by frame, slow-motion, forward and backward. Producers scripted the video with narration over it. They ran it with the natural sound up full. Over and over, the images streamed out of the television set. Local stations, networks, and twenty-four-hour cable operations wove the images into high-production segment opens. One Minneapolis station even used the file tape of the crash superimposed over some Twin City skyscrapers as a production technique, leaving the not-so-subtle reminder that, "It could happen here." The use of those images not only piqued already raw emotions, but gave us a sense that danger was all around.

In the days after the WTC attacks, Web sites warned that child could be affected by the repeated airing of the crash scene. Bab ter.com said, "Even if your children are very young, the con

165

commentary, frightening speculation, and repeated replaying of the disasters and military strikes on TV will only fuel their fears and insecurities, not to mention your own."

The September 11, 2001 attacks join a library of modern images that have seared their way into the viewer's consciousness; like the photograph of Elián González cowering from a federal agent, the Challenger space shuttle bursting into flames, or the home video of the Olympic Park blast rocking spectators in Atlanta. Over and over again, the pictures roll for days upon days of continuing coverage.

The repeated use of file tape can cause undue harm to people who have already suffered a profound loss. Sociologists and ethics experts say the overuse of images of tragedy or even the use of more routine images of generic crime scenes, fires, and other emergencies can skew viewers' perceptions of how much danger they are in when they travel or just venture outside their home. When TV stations use file tape over and over, it can also harm the people who are shown repeatedly in tragic circumstances or embarrassing situations, sometimes months or even years after the event occurred.

There are other reasons not to use file tape. Audience researchers find that the repeated use of file tape sends a signal that nothing is new, even if the stories contain new information.

In this chapter you will:

◇ Learn how file tape can skew the public's understanding about news events.

◇ See how the overuse or misuse of file tape can signal to the viewer that there is nothing new in your newscast or story.

◇ Understand how file tape can be deeply harmful to people who see themselves on the news night after night, sometimes years after an event, with no forewarning.

◇ Consider some guidelines for the use of file tape.

LAZY JOURNALISM

When jetliners crash, it is unquestionably "news" that journalists should print, and post online as the story is breaking and developing. The pictures help us to understand the size, the response to, and sometimes the causes of the accidents.

But when journalists continuously air or print pictures of such catastrophes, the public becomes concerned about "the wrong things," said Dr. Barry Glassner, a University of Southern California sociologist.

In Glassner's book, *The Culture of Fear,* he wrote: "Upon landing at the Baltimore airport, as he taxied to the terminal, the pilot of my flight from Los Angeles announced, 'The safest part of your journey is over. Drive home safely.'"[1] In an interview before the attacks on the World Trade Center, Dr. Glassner told me that since 1914, fewer than 13,000 people have died in airplane crashes.

"More than two times as many Americans lose their lives in auto crashes in a single year," Glassner said. Even considering the number of people who died on airlines September 11, air travel *is* far safer, per mile, than any other means of travel. Contrary to what you might believe based on what you see on the news, seven out of ten people who die in airplane crashes die in small general aviation planes, not commercial airliners.[2] One study commissioned by the Canadian Urban Transit Association found bike travel to be far more dangerous per kilometer traveled than any other mode of transportation. Bike riders have a fatality rate 200 times higher than bus, train, and light rail travel in Canada. But would we see file tape of a bicycle crash air over and over on television newscasts? It seems unlikely.

"When television news departments show those (file tapes) of disasters, it is lazy production," Glassner said. "One of the most important examples of how television stations misuse file tape is the Columbine footage, of those kids running from school. It has been shown thousands of times around the world. TV stations and networks showed those images over and over even at a time when school violence has been decreasing."

According to federal studies, the safest part of a child's day is when he or she is in school. "A child is more likely to be a victim of a violent crime in the community or at home than at school," a 1998 joint report by the Justice Department and the Education Departm[...]

[1]Dr. Barry Glassner, *The Culture of Fear* (New York: Basic Books,1999), 183.

[2]Aviation Accident Statistics 1982–1999, National Transportation Safety Board, *ww[...] aviation/Stats.htm*

said.[3] And yet, poll after national poll has shown that Americans believe schools are getting more dangerous, not less dangerous. A phone poll of 1,004 adults for *The Wall Street Journal* and NBC News revealed that 71 percent of Americans thought it was likely that a school shooting could happen in their community. A *Washington Post* poll conducted seven months after the shootings at Columbine High School revealed that 60 percent of respondents reported school violence as an issue that "worried them a great deal." According to two polls conducted by Gallup for the *USA Today*, respondents were 49 percent more likely to be fearful of schools in 1999 than in 1998. Polls showed that rural parents were the most fearful of school violence, even though the overwhelming majority of serious crime against or by youth occurs in cities.[4]

Glassner says the indiscriminate use of file tape showing Columbine High children running in fear months, even years, after the incident gives the wrong impression about what is happening in schools.

"Those tapes contain hot images that overwhelm the cold reality of statistics," Glassner said.

When journalists feed viewers a non-stop diet of video of people being arrested, carried off in body bags, or using drugs, the public naturally demands longer prison terms, stricter penalties, and more cops on the street. That barrage of images contradicts the Justice Department's own figures, which show violent crime and juvenile crime are on a steep decline in America and has been on that same track since the middle 1990s.[5]

Have the Courage Not to Use File Tape

Newsrooms should limit the use of file tape for other reasons, according to Deborah Potter, executive director of Newslab, a Washington, D.C.–based news laboratory that helps local stations tell more effective stories. Potter says audience researchers find that viewers see file tape as a signal that there is nothing new about the story, that they are seeing

—nal Report on School Safety, U.S. Department of Justice and U.S. Department of Education, r 1998; www.ed.gov/pubs/AnnSchoolRept98/execsum.html.

House Hype. Two years later," Justice Policy Institute/Children's Law Center, 1999; g/schoolhouse/mpelshh2exec.html.

e Trends 1 93–2000, United States Department of Justice, Bureau of Justice Sta- ww.ojp.usdoj.gov/bjs/glance/cv2.htm.

old news, even if the audio accompanying the file tape contains new information.

"One reason these pictures are so overused is that there is a desperation in TV newsrooms, a feeling we have to have a picture because we are TV. The research I have seen does not support the common newsroom rule that any video is better than none," Potter said.

The 2000 Camp David Middle East peace talks are a good example. The only video was of the leaders arriving. For days, viewers saw the same tape of the same three people wearing the same clothes, played over and over again.

"The viewers' natural reaction is, 'There must not be anything new, because they (the TV station) keeps showing me the same old stuff.'" Potter said. "One reason viewers say they tune out of TV news is because they get the sense that TV beats a story to death without providing any new information. A lot of this feeling is driven by file tape."

While file tape images can be numbing to viewers, they also can be shocking to the people whose images appear over and over again. How often do TV stations air video that includes clearly recognizable pictures of victims as video to illustrate a story about a crime bill making its way through the legislature. "These are real people; they are not file tape," Potter emphasizes.

File Tape Can Cause Harm

The stories of how we wreck people's lives with file tape are endless. Jim Heid, a freelance writer, tells about an incident involving his sister. "In late August 2001, a Pittsburgh TV station ran a news report covering changes proposed for county parks in western Pennsylvania. The changes dealt largely with pedestrian-safety issues, and were inspired by a horrific accident that occurred in a park last March: an elderly driver suffered a fatal aneurysm and his car careened into three pedestrians on a jogging trail, killing them. One of those pedestrians was my sister.

"As the news reporter spoke, a clip of the accident scene appeared. For several seconds, viewers saw a shot of the victims, their bodies draped with sheets, a crumpled Cadillac nearby. Unfortunately, my mother was watching.

"Later in the week, I called Mom to ask how she was doing. She itated, then admitted that she had recently had a 'bad day.' She ex how she had turned on the TV to get the morning news an image that brought back the worst tragedy of her eighty-two had not seen any pictures of the accident before, but now, she told me, the scene was burned into her brain.

"When the accident first occurred, my mother and the rest of our family were too preoccupied to watch the news. When a local paper ran a photo of the incident on its front page, my brother and I intercepted it so Mom wouldn't see it. Then, when my mother was least prepared for it, a TV station managed to aggravate a wound that shows little sign of healing."

The story that the TV station was doing that night was legitimate—pedestrian safety in public parks. But five months after a fatal accident, TV stations should consider alternatives to showing dead bodies draped in sheets. With each week that passes after the actual event, the threshold for using the graphic file images should get higher and higher. Heid even agrees that sometimes it is legitimate to show disturbing images, but he said, "I would also ask those news outlets to ask themselves two questions before broadcasting explicit images: Is it news, and is it necessary?"[6]

When I was a news director in Nashville, a guy called me on the phone one day. He asked, "Mr. Tompkins, is there any way I could choose not be on TV?" I asked what on earth he meant. He explained that a year or so earlier one of our camera crews had taken pictures of the man being arrested for drunken driving. The man was convicted and served his sentence. But for a year he said, every time there was a story about some lawmaker proposing new DUI laws, we would trot out the old video of this guy taking the field sobriety test. We used it so often, he said, that his friends and family knew every shot in the sequence. They could even identify his shoe as he touched the bumper with his foot at the police officer's direction.

I assured him I could do something about it. He had to call me two more times to complain. The video had become a virus in our tape morgue. It would show up endlessly until we got in there and edited it out of every story in which it had ever been used to keep it from being used in another story by mistake. He was no longer a man to us. He had become file tape.

It took our chief editor an entire day to track down all of the stories which we had used this man's image. We blacked over the file tape

"My Sister's Dead Body Is No Longer News," *Newsweek* (September 17, 2001), 12.

images in our tape morgue and kept intact only the one story in which he appeared the first time, being arrested.

A Missouri television newsroom showed me a piece of videotape about a fight that erupted outside a courtroom. One woman socked another woman right in the nose and, as it happened, the camera was rolling. The blow to the face is loud and hard. Beginning to end, the whole incident lasted five seconds. Nobody was charged, and nobody was seriously hurt. The TV station decided not to air the assault since it had little bearing on the case going on in the courtroom. It was just bad blood between two women. Years later, while the same, usually careful TV station was producing a story about rage in America, a journalist found the unused file tape and included it in his story. The station had methodically made a decision not the use the tape the first time, but once the tape became "file tape" it was there to be freely used without discussion. They only used it because it was "great video."

GUIDELINES FOR USING FILE TAPE

Here are some guidelines to help newsrooms make ethical decisions about how, when, and how often to use file tape:

- What is the journalistic purpose for using file tape? Ask each time you use an image: "What truths does this image tell that would not be told if we didn't use the picture?"
- How does the truth of the file picture measure up to the potential harm the continued use of the image might cause to others who were involved in the story?
- How clear is the viewer that the file tape is, in fact, historic, not shot today?
- What "harm" could the use of file video cause to the viewer by repeatedly showing disturbing pictures?
- What discussion does your newsroom have about how long graphic images are "news" and when they become "file"?
- What obligation do you have to notify the people who are shown in file tape that you intend to use their images again, sometimes weeks or months after an incident?
- What guidelines does your newroom have about the use of tape in promotions?

REMEMBER: File tape should be used sparingly. Newsrooms should establish guidelines for when and how it is appropriate for journalists to include file tape in their stories. Journalists should ask whether file tape is necessary to telling the story. If it is necessary, the journalist should look for ways to minimize the harm that might come to others by showing file images.

Chapter 10

The Power of Enterprise Reporting

"Just because your voice reaches halfway around the world doesn't mean you are wiser than when it reached only to the end of the bar."

EDWARD R. MURROW (1908–1965)

THE COMPLAINT I HEAR MOST often from viewers is "all TV newscasts are pretty much the same." It is rare to find a television market where the majority of viewers say they have a strong preference for one station over another. And those preferences usually center around an individual anchor or an anchor team. There are some exceptions. WSVN-TV in Miami carved out a market niche with its fast-paced breaking news style. But mostly, *journalists*, not the *public*, see the differences among stations.

In October 2001, I hosted a town meeting of TV viewers in St. Petersburg, Florida. One man stood up to say, "I can switch from one station to another and they all have the same stories in the same order. It is all the same; it is like they called each other to decide what they would put on their news that night." The sameness of the news could be an important reason why local television news viewership is dropping like a stone. The Pew Research Center says that the number of people who said they "regularly watched" local news dropped from 64 percent in 1993 to 56 percent in 2000.

The single most important thing any television station could do stand out in the marketplace is to put more emphasis on enterprise rep ing. I think of enterprise reporting as any story that looks beyon "what" to find the "so what," "how often," and "why." The story m with an event, but the enterprise reporter goes beyond the eve

173

context and meaning. Enterprise is at the heart of great journalism. Sadly, I find it missing from many newscasts as I travel coast to coast.

In this chapter I will:

◇ Help you find ways to turn the morning editorial meeting into the most important hour of the news day. You will find ways to use the morning meeting to celebrate and encourage enterprise in your newsroom.

◇ Help you find ways to turn the ordinary non-visual story into a memorable enterprise story.

◇ Help you find new stories in old beats.

◇ Tell you about some of my favorite story idea gold mines on the Internet.

ENTERPRISE FROM THE START: MORNING MEETINGS

Exasperated news directors ask me, "Where have all of the great stories gone? Why don't reporters seem to find news? How can our station find stories nobody else finds? Why don't reporters and producers contribute any ideas about what we should cover?" These questions and hundreds more like them all point to the same trouble spot in TV newsrooms. Newsrooms need to rethink the morning meeting. The old saying "garbage in, garbage out" was never more applicable. If your morning meeting is unproductive, unimaginative, and non-inclusive, your newscast will show it.

That crucial hour or so does more to set the tone of a newsroom than any other hour of the day, including the evening news hour(s). That is often the only time in the day when the newsroom meets as a team to discuss values and ideas and, by extension, to develop its culture and style. Often, it offers the most one-on-one conversation that reporters and producers have with newsroom managers. How can we make this important time more useful?

GET WHAT YOU INSPECT MORE THAN YOU EXPECT

reporting should take shape in the daily morning editorial morning meetings often begin with an assignment editor reciting the event calendar, but great morning meetings don't end there. Planned events should be the *minimum* of what a newsroom should consider for the day's coverage.

How would you describe the tone of your morning meeting? Is it, "Here is what we are going to do. Now, let's go feed the beast."? Or does it begin with, "We are looking for the strongest stories today. We have some events and topics in mind, but if your ideas are stronger, let's go for it."

Producers and news managers must honor strong enterprise ideas by giving them airtime and resources. Back where I grew up in Kentucky, there was a wonderful saying, "Saying ain't doing." Newsrooms generate more enterprise stories when they "inspect"; they hold every member of the department accountable for enterprising stories rather than just "expect"—when they merely *say* they want more enterprise stories. The surest way to kill morning meetings is to "talk a good game" in the meeting then spend the rest of the day chasing mindless spot news that doesn't affect your viewers.

This means that for stations to increase their enterprise reporting, they would have to make a decision NOT to chase every minor breaking news story and not be driven by what they see on the competitor's channel.

A newsroom that honors enterprise sets its own tone—it has decided what it stands for and makes coverage decisions accordingly. A newsroom that enterprises is proactive, not reactive. A newsroom that enterprises leads the audience toward important issues. A newsroom that enterprises finds topics that others seldom cover and includes people who are otherwise seldom seen in the newscasts. Stations that do not enterprise but cover events often are the ones that include the same old, tired PR flacks, cops, and "suits" because they are the ones who hold news conferences or show up at events and crime scenes.

Great newsrooms cultivate a "forward thinking" atmosphere. In these newsrooms, part of a reporter's job description is to file daily story notes at the end of the shift. Reporters drop these notes in a computer file that can be accessed by anyone in the newsroom. The story note can contain ideas for follow-ups or ideas for future stories. If a repor covers a crime or an arrest today, for example, the story note might tain suggestions about how to follow the case. Maybe the crime in an unusual weapon, was in a high- or low-crime area, or ha stumped. If the case involves an arrest, the story note shoul when the case will move forward in court. These notes can be valuable if a reporter is working "nightside" and the "dayside" crews will need to follow up.

Great newsrooms also reward achievement. News managers should talk about and reward enterprise during performance reviews. And there are other ways to encourage enterprise.

"We invite anyone who saw something great on our air the day before to bring it to the morning meeting," says Lane Michaelson, news director at WTSP-TV, Tampa. When he was a news director at KTHV-TV, Little Rock, he started rebuilding his newsroom by playing a "daily win" story in the morning meeting every day. The "daily win" might be a standup, a use of natural sound, a well-thought-out graphic, or a remarkably clear lead. "We wanted to celebrate the little achievements that add up to a better newscast. It takes a minute or two, but it sets a positive tone for the day."

Place and Space

Where does your meeting take place? Meetings in news directors' offices with closed doors send a clear signal: "Don't bother us; we will tell you what you are covering when we finish." How can your newsroom find a more inviting place to meet that sends a clear signal to reporters, photojournalists, and anyone else who can contribute to the pool of story ideas for the day?

Does your morning meeting space include a computer that is connected to the Internet? Many morning meetings get bogged down in guessing games and speculation when a quick online search could give you the nugget needed to make a story doable. The morning meeting should be a fairly sacred place. It is an hour or ninety minutes when important work gets done. The morning meeting is not the place to read the morning paper. It should be newsroom policy that every newsroom employee should read a daily newspaper before he or she reports for work. I mean that. Every reporter, every editor, every producer, everyone should read that day's newspaper if they want to work in a newsroom.

Include Many Voices

in the newsroom when you meet? Often, newsroom editorial begin even before photojournalists and reporters arrive for the day. If you shifted the start time of your meeting by fifteen minutes, could you get more voices involved in the discussion?

"If you want the voices and ideas of photojournalists, you have to hold the meeting when photojournalists are in the building, and you have to take the time to hear what they are saying," says Linda Angelle, KXAS-TV, Dallas, photojournalist and past president of the National Press Photographers Association. "If a photojournalist pitches an idea one day and it is ignored or shot down, that photographer will think twice before pitching an idea again."

The morning meeting should welcome online editors, graphic artists, and promotion people. The sooner they know what is on the menu, the more effectively they can support the day's news.

Look around your meeting table. How diverse are the people in age, race, ethnicity, experience in the market, marital status, and job description? If the meeting is packed with white men in suits, how can you expect to think of stories that minorities and women want to see? If the morning meeting is packed with thirty-somethings but nobody over age forty, how can you expect to know what your most loyal viewers, who are over age fifty, want to see tonight? Does anyone in the room have kids? (Thirty percent of your viewers do.)

EFFICIENT DOES NOT MEAN EFFECTIVE

Nobody has time to waste on an unproductive meeting. Reporters and photojournalists want to get out the door and start shooting their story(s). Producers want to start scanning the wires, writing, and searching feeds for interesting material.

But efficiency does not always equal effectiveness. Don't hurry through the meeting with such speed that people don't have time to pitch a great idea. And a short morning meeting that ends in confusion about "who is doing what" isn't effective. Newsrooms spend a lot of time redirecting crews and thinking up fallback plans at midday when morning meetings fail to include a full discussion of a story idea. The morning meeting is an investment in the rest of the day.

"The daily meeting is crucial to how I do my work," says repor Boyd Huppert, KARE11-TV, Minneapolis. "That is the most im tant half-hour or hour of the day. If we don't get our plans right the rest of the day is a mess."

Be prompt; start your meeting on time. Meetings that always start late tend to train participants to come in late.

Can We Adjourn?

More than once, I have temporarily adjourned a morning meeting because it was clear we did not have enough good ideas on the table to go forward with a productive news day. By adjourning for a half-hour, we were able to make another round of calls to sources, and check wires and Internet sites to find better leads. Newsrooms should have the courage to stop the meeting if it is going nowhere. By making that suggestion, even if you are not the boss, you send a signal that your newsroom has a standard for quality that you will not compromise.

Why Are We Meeting?

Remember, there are three reasons for editorial meetings:

1. **Find the best stories.** KCNC-TV, Denver, news director Angie Kucharski says her morning meeting focuses first on the "lead or probable lead" for each show. "We move on to the stories that will show up at each quarter-hour in our news block. We think of the 4 to 6 P.M. news block as having eight quarter-hour pillars that hold it up. As part of our strategy to hold audience and ratings, we want strong stories on each quarter hour." Kucharski says before her team developed this way of assigning stories in the morning, "We handed out desserts, salads, and breads, but our newscast didn't have enough steak. Now we make sure we have enough meat in our shows first. It begins in the morning meeting."

2. **Create a culture.** The morning meeting is the first and best opportunity newsroom leaders have to create and cultivate a newsroom culture that honors enterprise reporting. Celebrate wins, honor creative ideas, and listen. Great newsrooms often post a statement of news principles or a mission statement in the morning meeting room.

3. **Collaborate.** The morning meeting is the best time to take ordinary stories and, through collaboration, make them better. A morning meeting is the perfect place to have a quick discussion about how to localize a mundane but important topic or bring broad story ideas into tighter focus.

Remember: Morning meetings set the tone for the newsroom's day. Newsrooms should develop a culture of enterprise reporting, valuing stories that explain the "why, how often, and what about that" questions as much as they value stories that only address "what happened."

HOW TO ENTERPRISE

SEEK THE IDEAS OF OTHERS

More voices add richness, diversity, and perspective to your ideas. How can you talk to more people who might have great ideas for stories? My favorite sources included a pharmacist, a pediatrician, a real-estate developer, a mechanic, a junkyard owner, an aviation expert, a veterinarian, a grocery store manager, and a county jailer (in Kentucky there really is an elected position, county jailer). I had long friendships with a Catholic priest who ran a homeless shelter and a preschool teacher who worked in a tough part of Nashville.

I would ask them what they were seeing that I should know about. I would ask them what was new in their business. When a prescription drug started getting newspaper headlines, I would ask my pharmacist friend if the drug was really new, or if it was just publicity hype. I would ask my mechanic friend all sorts of automotive questions including questions about recalls and safety issues. My friend who owned an auto junkyard was a non-stop source of information about criminal investigations because cops were constantly dropping by telling him to be on the lookout for stuff that had been stolen or used in a crime.

My homebuilder/developer friend knew all about the city's planning, zoning, arbor, water, and sewage laws. Another developer under fire for planning to tear down an old but well-known apartment complex. Neighborhood groups protested against the demolition the retail development plans. My friend helped me understand sobering economics of renovating such an old apartment building. My friend had no personal interest in the apartment project, so he became a good source of background advice for our stories.

In the cold winter of 1986, parish priest Father Charles Strobel noticed families spending the night in cars in the church parking lot, turning the engines on and off during the night to run the heaters, then coming to the rectory door in the morning and asking for money for gasoline. Unable to sleep at night while these people were suffering, he decided to open the church cafeteria as a shelter; and with the help of church volunteers, it stayed open from Thanksgiving time through Easter.

Father Strobel was one of the first people I encountered after I moved to Nashville. We met at a Saturday morning public hearing about homelessness. After the meeting, he took me to his church soup kitchen to meet his clients. He wanted me to talk with them without a camera. He knew all of the hardcore homeless people by name and helped me know and begin to understand some of them. Father Strobel never called me seeking publicity for his street ministry, even though publicity probably would have brought in more money. But his door was always open to me to come in and ask questions as I worked on stories about poverty, repeat criminal offenders, and life on the street.

One of the best places I knew to get a reality check was Marva Southhall's East Nashville preschool classroom. Like most reporters, I was always in a hurry, so sometimes my visits would just last a half-hour. I would find a chair in the corner of the Caldwell School classroom and listen to the children. They lived in the city's toughest neighborhood. Marva's class sometimes practiced "Code 1000" drills. The drill involved the children jumping out of their chairs, lying face down on the floor, and covering their heads with their hands in the event there was gunfire outside Marva's classroom window. One of her classroom windows was pockmarked with bullet holes.

Marva told me heartbreaking stories of her children, who often did not recognize their real names, just their nicknames. Some children had no idea how to hug or be hugged. Many lacked enough self-esteem to look Marva in the eye. One young boy had so little self-esteem he could say a word out loud without covering his mouth with his hand.

Marva's classroom always reminded me what was important in life. constantly pushed me to do more stories about children and education strongly urged me to become a teacher myself. As you can see, the preschoolers were not the only ones who learned in Marva South-hall's class. I'll bet there is somebody just like her in your town waiting for you to walk through the classroom door.

SEEK VOICES AND FACES SELDOM SEEN ON TV

Enterprising reporters ask, "Who do we always talk to on this story?" Then they ask, "Who do we *never* talk to?" "Who has a stake in this story other than the usual people we interview?" The seldom-heard-from, the under-covered people are almost always more interesting than those who appear on the news every night. Go find them.

Steve Weinberg, an investigative writer and one of the founders of Investigative Reporters and Editors, Inc. (IRE) told me that he joined a bowling league, in part, to meet more people. He said he was surprised at the diversity in a bowling alley.

You will not connect with your community merely by living there for a long time. We all develop migratory patterns of driving the same route to work, eating at the same restaurants, and shopping in the same places year after year. Journalists must understand that they are different from the communities they seek to serve.

Peter Brown, editor of the Sunday Insight section for the *Orlando Sentinel*, wanted to know how different journalists are from the public. "It doesn't make a difference if the guy who repairs your air conditioner lives the life you do. But journalists' view of the world determines not just how they cover a story, but what stories they cover."

Brown and pollster Bill Hamilton surveyed 500 residents and 478 journalists in five American cities: Dayton, Ohio; Tulsa, Oklahoma; Syracuse, New York; Roanoke, Virginia; and Chico/Redding, California. Mind you, these were not *New York Times, Washington Post,* or network correspondents. These were working journalists in medium-sized towns.

While 18 percent of the public earned $50,000 or more, 42 percent of the journalists did. Thirty percent of the journalists said they had to make $40,000 just to make ends meet, compared with 12 percent of the public who said so. Replies show that, compared with other Americans, journalists are more likely to live in upscale neighborhoods, have maids, own a Mercedes, and trade stock; they're less likely to go to church, volunteer work, or put down roots in a community. Journalists are o represented in ZIP codes where residents are twice as likely as other Americans to rent foreign movies, drink Chablis, own an espresso maker, and read such magazines as *Architectural Digest* and *Food & Wine*.[1]

How many people in your newsroom belong to the American Legion or the Kiwanis or go to prayer breakfasts? If your newsroom is anything like the ones Brown polled or the ones I have worked in, the answer will be "none or next to none." Journalists must make a stronger effort to connect with people who are not like themselves.

In the mid-1990s, Nashville saw a big construction boom because of two huge downtown projects. At the same time, the city noticed a significant increase in Hispanic laborers. I wanted to find ways for my newsroom to serve the growing Latino population and started attending Hispanic Resource Council meetings in Nashville. I met a well-connected Hispanic attorney and a Hispanic dentist who helped me understand the complexities of health care for undocumented residents. I did not join the council because, as a journalist, I worried that one day I might have to report on issues the council was involved in.

But I found the meetings valuable when the Immigration and Naturalization Service made a high-profile roundup of Latino workers who were helping build the new city arena. Without those sources, we would have done what other reporters did, rely almost solely on the INS's version of the story. Instead, we were able to show a more complete picture of hard-working people who were doing the best they could to provide for their families. We also came to understand how important these workers were to our community, which had low unemployment and a huge need for skilled laborers.

Social workers at the Nashville Housing Authority helped photojournalist Mark O'Neill and me connect with the small Cambodian, Vietnamese, and Ethiopian communities of our town when we wanted to tell stories about Nashville slumlords who took advantage of poor non-English speaking immigrants.

One of The Poynter Institute's experts on issues of diversity, Aly Colón, encourages reporters to find places where people are likely to stop and talk, mingle, and share information about themselves. Barber shops, beauty salons, community centers, and ethnic restaurants are what Colón calls "listening posts."

---

n Leo, "Those Darn Readers: The gap between reporters and the general public is huge," *News and World Report* (April 24, 2000): 16.

"Some of the most informed people in a community are often funeral directors, day-care center directors, health clinic workers, and neighborhood association presidents," he says. But he cautions journalists to use a variety of community listening posts to avoid becoming a pawn of factions or prominent sources in any community.

Journalists should get out in public without their notebooks and cameras. In my workshops I often ask producers and reporters how many of them have ever been to a school PTA meeting that they were not covering. Almost no hands go up. I ask how many have visited a school just to learn what is going on in schools these days. No hands go up. You get the point. Journalists are not at all like the people they seek to serve. TV journalists could narrow the distance between themselves and the public if they would find listening posts in their community such as day-care centers, community restaurants, and barber shops where everyday people gather.

An anchor with whom I worked, Demetria Kalodimos, hit the road one day, as she often did before she started her regular anchor shift, to deliver a luncheon speech in rural middle Tennessee. On her way home, she stopped for gasoline at a country market, a farming community listening post that she knew well. Demetria is not only a strong anchor but is a skilled reporter who knows her coverage area thoroughly, so when she saw a number of signs written in Spanish she knew it was unusual. Like many rural Tennessee counties, this one was nearly all white and certainly not known for being multi-ethnic. She started asking questions.

Demetria learned that middlemen, who were acting as labor recruiters, were encouraging Mexican and Central American migrant workers to work on Tennessee and Kentucky tobacco farms. It was backbreaking labor that usually paid cash. The migrants had begun taking jobs in the important tree and shrubbery nurseries in middle Tennessee as well. Our newsroom was completely unaware of their immigration, but it was becoming common knowledge to our viewers in rural communities who saw the migrants at the country stores, gas stations, and coin laundries. Rural hospitals noticed an increase in migrant farm worker injuries. Some injured or sick workers were too frightened of deportation to seek medical treatment.

Demetria discovered that the workers were living in rundo unheated shacks. Often a dozen or more migrants shared one f room, while their white bosses lived in big comfortable farm nearby. Our newsroom decided that the only way we could know exactly how the migrant system worked was to do something we rarely did, go undercover. Demetria allowed me to pose as a farmer looking for workers as we set about learning how middlemen recruited the immigrants to work at the farms. Demetria's series, "Hard Luck Harvest," aired right in the middle of the fall tobacco auction season. We showed how there was no reason for farmers to take such advantage of the migrants since there were many legal government-sponsored programs that would help the farmers provide proper housing and health care. Farmers, social workers, and community leaders gathered at rural meetings to do something about the horrible living conditions and other concerns. The investigation won a National Headliner Award. All that, just because one journalist noticed a few signs written in Spanish, and was curious enough to ask questions. That is "enterprise reporting."

SEEK TRUTHS

In the "Hard Luck Harvest" series, as in most stories, the more we learned about the issue, the more sides to the story we discovered. We learned that there were many stakeholders in this story including:

- the farmers
- the workers
- the middlemen
- the hospitals
- health clinics
- the communities
- the families
- other migrants
- social workers
- lawyers
- federal state and local lawmakers
- the INS
- other workers
- and, of course, the television station

We could have easily gotten bogged down in the pro and con story he Immigration and Naturalization Service versus the farmer. But ould have missed other vital parts of the story, including the story lives, hopes, and dreams of workers themselves, many of whom rking to send money back to Mexico to support their families.

Enterprising reporters don't focus just on the extremes of "anti" and "pro." How could you find new voices to cover the battle about abortion, capital punishment, and stories about gun control or taxation? The social activists on those issues have fax machines, PR agencies, and news conferences. But the people most closely affected by those issues are seldom in the stories.

ASK BETTER QUESTIONS

Valerie Hyman of BetterNews (*www.betternews.com*) says that once a reporter finishes an interview, he or she should ask a few more questions to help with the story. Questions include:

- What else should I know?
- Who else should I talk to?
- If you were me, where would you go next?
- What kind of records or pictures are there of this?

AVOID THE PACK; GO WHERE THE STORY IS GOING NEXT

If you want to find stories, go where the other stations aren't. Keep asking yourself, "What is most likely to happen next in this story? How can I get ahead of the story, not always react to events?" I think journalists worry too much about what the other stations are reporting and not enough about what they themselves are reporting. Inform yourself about what the "other guys" are covering, but be guided by your own journalistic principles and your newsroom's thoughtful vision. Cover stories that matter to your viewers. Don't just include stories in your newscast or soundbites in your stories because the other station has them. Remember, it is good to be different from the pack. You should stand out in the viewers' minds, not blend into the background noise.

TALK TO PEOPLE WHOM OTHERS OVERLOOK

Some of my best sources were oddballs, eccentrics, and those who ha an ax to grind; but it did not make them wrong. I remember Dora M cer, a colorful woman who lived in rural Kentucky. I first heard f her in 1985, when she called and wrote to our newsroom saying her cows were deformed. She sounded like a nut.

One day we dropped by to see her. Sure enough, her cattle were staggering around. They had sores on their mouths. We noticed that the cows drank from a nearby waterway called Mud River. I learned, through months of interviews and record checks, that Rockwell International's nearby die-cast factory accidentally released PCBs and other chemicals into the river. We found state records that showed inspectors had been concerned about chemical leaks from the plant as early as the 1950s. We found records of fish kills near the plant, and we interviewed frustrated state inspectors who had spent years quietly documenting the slow death of the river. There is no scientific proof that Rockwell hurt Dora's cows. But her questions started our investigation. By 1996, ten years later, the company spent more than $20 million cleaning the river.[2] We never would have looked into the story if we had not listened to Dora's seemingly crazy claims.

In my experience, whistleblowers, and crusaders are often angry enough to become packrats. They save scraps of evidence that will prove their case. One guy I found had been fighting the Tennessee Tombigbee waterway project for twenty years. The $2 billion project was the single most expensive public works project in American history, and it was a boondoggle from the very start.

Randall Grace grew frustrated and angry about the government's pie-in-the-sky promises that that the Tenn-Tom would deliver prosperity to impoverished Mississippi and Alabama. Grace gave up the fight that took a decade of his young adulthood and built a rustic and secluded log cabin in the wooded hills of Tennessee. He also built a little shed next to the house.

When I finally found him and spent some time with him talking about his struggle against the Corps of Engineers, I noticed the little shed. I asked him what he kept in it. Grace lit up. He had crammed box upon cardboard box of records into the shed. I dug around to find hundreds of pages of clippings, letters, and what looked to be thousands of photographic slides of the waterway before, during, and after the construction that had cost more than twice what the Corps had promised Congress it would. It was like manna from heaven for me. I could have bear-hugged the guy.

My photojournalist friend Pat Slattery and I once heard about an ┤derly woman who had spent her whole life fighting the Tennessee Val-

─────────
well International Corp. v. Vance Wilhite, et al., Nos. 1997-CA-000188-MR, 1997-CA-
ᵃ-MR and 1997-CA-000348-MR, Ky. App.

ley Authority. When we caught up with Corrine Whitehead, we found a firebrand of a woman who had not only saved hundreds of photographs and newspaper clippings that chronicled her lifelong railing against government excesses, she had indexed the clippings and correspondence in files by date and topic. Corrine's voice reminded me of Katharine Hepburn's. Corrine wore a shirt collar stylishly flipped up in the back, the way Bogart flipped up his trench coat collar in *Casablanca.* A form of polio weakened Corrine when she was a young woman. Her hands shook as she slowly flipped through her files with us. We tried not to be too gleeful as we sat in the middle of her stash, but we wondered how it could have happened that nobody had ever listened to her story before.

The Kennedy administration ordered Corrine and her neighbors off their homesteads in order to build two big hydroelectric dams and two large lakes. Any land that was not flooded would become a public recreation area that the government said would never be developed. For thirty years she was a thorn in TVA's side. She became one of those gadfly eccentrics who shows up at every public meeting, and reporters curiously avoid.

In the 1990s, when TVA's budgets got tight, the agency wanted to lease the very land it had ordered Corrine to vacate. Condo developers and gas station quick markets would be free to set up shop on the land the government promised would remain non-commercial forever. Corrine's files allowed us to prove the government made promises to the people of rural western Kentucky that the land would never be developed. After being hammered on the news day after day, TVA backed off its plans.

Listen to people like Corrine, Randall, and Dora. They have hearts of gold and closets full of papers you need. Be willing to interview anyone if they have a great story.

DON'T QUIT STORIES TOO SOON

Return to stories to see what has happened. Viewers love follow-ups. Just about the time you are sick of a story, viewers figure out there *is* a story. Television station researchers tell me that in many markets, especially big-city markets, the most loyal viewers rarely watch more th[a] two and a half newscasts per week. Viewers get frustrated when stati[on] cover an arrest and do not follow up on the court proceedings. [They] don't track every little event the way journalists do. They don't ev[er]y criminal suspect and the crimes the suspect allegedly was in[...]

in the way a producer, having written ten versions of the story for ten newscasts and news cut-ins in two days, knows that person. *We overestimate what viewers know—we underestimate how smart they are.*

But journalists must be careful when enterprising follow-up stories. With breaking news, victims can literally be scared speechless. Don't be lulled into thinking that the effects of trauma simply disappear with the passage of time. Be careful when you contact victims for follow-ups.

Michigan State University associate journalism professor Sue Carter has studied how media coverage affects crime victims and offers some advice about follow-up stories:

• **Anniversary and update stories.** It is a mistake to assume that victims do not suffer pain ten, twenty, or even fifty years after the incident. The anniversary itself often stirs up troubling feelings, so be prepared when asking for and conducting an interview.

• **Unsolved crimes.** Try to make it your policy never to run a story about an unsolved crime without notifying the victim or the family first. Particularly in the case of murder, surviving family members feel blindsided when they are not warned that a story will appear about a new suspect or as part of a feature on unsolved crimes.

• **A special word on terminology.** Victims who have had a chance to think about their experience often have strong feelings about "loaded" words such as victim, survivor, and closure. Ask if they mind being called a victim. Many victims bristle at being asked if they have achieved closure; the implication is that they are a failure if they say no, and many would argue that you may someday forgive but will never forget. A better question might be, "How do you feel about the question of closure?"

BUILD A DIVERSE ROLODEX

I can usually tell how good reporters are by how fat their "little black books" are and by how quickly they can find important phone numbers. Enterprising journalists make certain their Rolodexes or electronic personal organizers include a rich mix of sources including racial, ethnic, gender, religious, and political minorities. Some people collect dolls or coins. Great enterprising journalists collect business cards and phone numbers. I like the electronic address organizers but one day, when our newsroom computers failed because of a big storm, I came to appreciate the reporters who keep phone numbers stowed in little address books stored away in their pockets or purse. I make a paper backup for my entire electronic name and address files. Those files represent a lifetime of work, and I don't trust them to any machine.

DRIVE A NEW ROUTE HOME

Your community is constantly changing. It changes with the season, with the ups and downs of the economy. It even changes from what it is in the daylight to what it becomes at night. Discover your community's changing complexion by taking a new route home once in a while. Mark Anderson, the chief photojournalist at KSTP-TV, Minneapolis, tells photojournalists to drive with their windows open so they can hear stories. It is quite a piece of advice from somebody who lives in ice-cold Minnesota, but I have seen stories he found that way, including a story about a remarkable street musician whom Mark heard as he drove through downtown St. Paul.

WRITE THANK-YOU LETTERS

CBS News correspondent Byron Pitts carries postage stamps and thank-you notes in his briefcase. After he finishes interviewing people, he drops them a short note of thanks for their help. Lots of journalists would not dare go back to some towns where they did stories the locals hated. But Byron takes great care to treat his interview subjects as humans. Sometimes his subjects send him new stories because they know he will treat them sensitively and with great respect.

It is also a great idea to send thank-you notes to your news director when he or she gives you some extra time or resources to produce a story. Send a note to producers who grant you a little extra airtime to tell your story or to photojournalists who bust their hump to get the extra shot or remarkable sound. Thank-you notes are so much more personal and meaningful than e-mails or e-cards.

REMEMBER: Find community listening posts to inform your reporting. Be open to sources whom others ignore or dismiss. Seek out new sources of information. Follow up stories. Viewers don't watch as often as you think.

A Better Way of Covering Catastrophe, Cops, and Crime

I have no problem with covering significant crime stories in the news. I do see too much crime coverage on local news and most of the coverage I see is about the crime, not about the larger issues the individual act might represent.

In 2001 The Project for Excellence in Journalism watched TV newscasts from forty-three TV stations in fourteen cities. "The tone [of local news] is generally chatty, breathless and superficial," the study reports. The researchers also discovered:

- Forty percent of stories last thirty seconds or less
- One in four stories is about crime, law, or courts
- Fewer than 1 percent of stories could be called "investigative"
- Health stories outnumber all other social issues by 32 percent
- There are as many stories about bizarre occurrences (8 percent), as there are about civic institutions.

Two topics that were barely covered are the fine arts, which accounted for only twenty-four stories out of the 6,000 studied, and poverty/welfare, which accounted for only nine stories.[3]

I suspect in some cities, crime coverage is much higher than 25 percent. How do journalists justify that level of coverage? It is easy to drive by a murder scene and take pictures. Crime coverage, as many stations think of it, requires little manpower and little investment of time, and many newsrooms believe that viewers want and like crime coverage. But society pays a heavy price for the skewed coverage. Look at the chart on the following page from the United States Justice Department Bureau of Justice Statistics.[4]

Notice a sharp decline in violent crime in the middle 1990s to the lowest levels the country has seen in thirty years. What possible justification is there then for a sharp increase in crime coverage? **Stations should cover crime responsibly.** Don't exaggerate the size of the problem or severity of crime. For the last decade nationwide, violent crimes have dropped, so how did it come about that by mid-decade 62 percent of us described ourselves as "truly desperate" about crime,

___

dy for the Project of Excellence, *Columbia Journalism Review* (November/December 2001).
au of Justice Statistics, National Crime Victimization Survey, 1973–96.

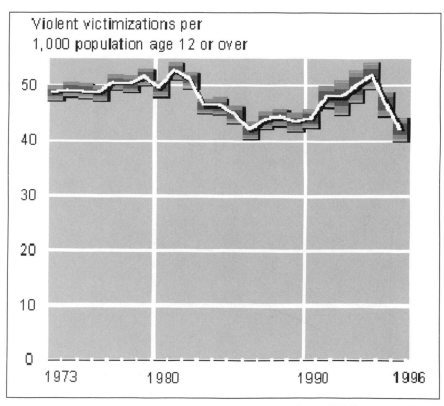

Source: U.S. Department of Justice

almost twice as many as in the late 1980s when crime rates were truly higher? National surveys say most people formed their opinions because they "saw it on the news" while only 22 percent cited personal experience.[5]

Exaggerated coverage has the potential to encourage viewers to disconnect with their community, turn inward for safety and shut the community out of their lives.

But journalists have a duty to alert viewers to real threats. I wonder how many journalists wrote twenty-second copy stories about wrecks, even fatal crashes that involved Ford Explorers with Firestone tires, before David Raziq, Anna Werner, and Chris Henao at KHOU-TV, Houston, started their investigation in the fall of 1999. By late summer 2000, that investigation led to the largest automotive parts recall in the history of the car. Raziq told me the fundamental shift occurred wher

---

[5]Glassner, *The Culture of Fear*, xxi.

the KHOU team moved beyond covering the accidents and started asking the enterprising questions, "Why is this happening? Where is it happening? What is behind all of this?"[6] The KHOU team mapped the Ford Explorer/Firestone tire accident reports and quickly saw that the accidents were occurring all over America. The number of cases, they said, were an indication that this was not a few acts of bad luck but a systemic problem with either the vehicle, the tires, or both.

The KHOU team sets a strong example for how to cover crime too. In November 2001, Raziq started asking questions about another issue: rape. He asked, "Were women more vulnerable to rape in some areas of Houston than others? And if so, what was it about these areas that was attracting predatory rapists?" Raziq got his hands on three years of rape reports from the City of Houston Police Department. Then he plotted the incidents on a map of the city (on the following page). Certain areas jumped out with very high levels of sexual assault.

The investigative team was surprised to find that one of the worst sections of town was an upscale area of the city (located near a country club) with eighty-nine reported rapes. In fact, in that same "rape zone" there was also a "path" of sexual assaults stretching up one street and connecting to another and then another street, extending for miles. Since KHOU's broadcasts, some criminal investigators are now calling that area "rape row."

Next, KHOU's team went on-site to these hot spots to see what could be attracting would-be rapists. Bringing along a well-known crime and security expert, the team found many spots had easy access to nearby freeways, high concentrations of apartment complexes with little or no security, poor lighting, and gates that didn't work. What was worse, KHOU said, "When rapes did occur at one of these properties, usually the other residents living there were not told about them." To help solve that problem, KHOU posted its rape database online so viewers could check on the history of their neighborhood. Within two hours of broadcast, viewers flooded the Web site with more than 5,200 page hits.

LOOK FOR THE STORY BEHIND THE STORY

Enterprise reporting and thinking plays out in the decisions that newsrooms make every day. It will show up in the way you treat people who

---

iq, Henao, and Werner interviewed by author August 2000.

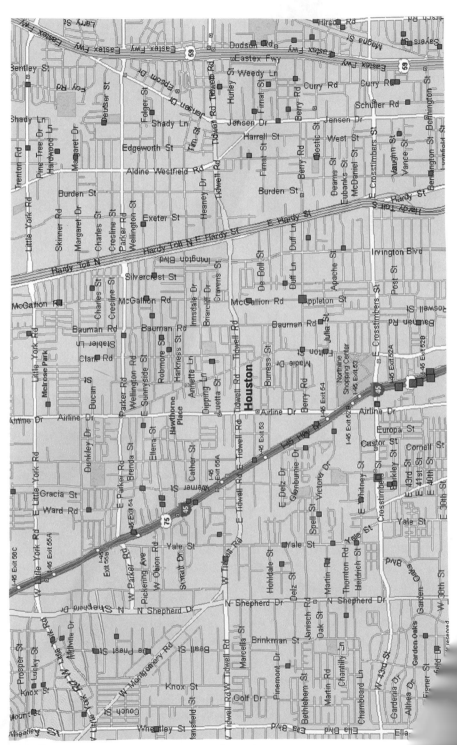

Source:

call your newsroom. I learned that lesson even before I worked in a newsroom.

In my hometown of Caldwell County, Kentucky, the school board found the money to build a new bare-bones high school for our rural community. But in its cost cutting, the county didn't earmark the several hundred dollars needed to install a flagpole outside the school. Some friends of mine and I, with the urging of our always-patriotic science teacher Dale Faughn, decided we should do something about that.

We called a local construction company and asked it to donate a load of concrete. We sold Tootsie Rolls and Hershey bars and raised enough money to buy a flagpole. We leaned on the local VFW to procure a big flag that had flown over the state Capitol.

With all of that done, I mustered up the courage to make a "long-distance call" to the local television station. The station was fifty miles away, but it was only one of three stations that the people in my town could pick up on their antennas. Unless you invested in a big antenna for your home, it was the *only* station you could watch.

I practiced my pitch over and over before making the call. I was sure I could convince the TV station to drive to our school and do a story about our little act of patriotism. On the other end of the phone was the voice of a harried producer or assignment desk manager who, ten seconds into our conversation, had the idea stuck in his mind "this is a story about a flag pole." There was a certain "thanks, but no thanks" quality to his voice.

If he had asked, he would have seen the story through a very different lens; the lens through which we were looking. As high school seniors, we had just seen two big events occur. The war in Vietnam had just ended. Only a few months earlier, my classmates and I were eligible for the draft. From the time I was five years old, Americans had been fighting in Vietnam. It was cool to hate the government. It was cool to question authority. Now, there was no war and these country boys were no longer in danger of being drafted.

My buddies Mark VanHooser, Jeff Alsobrook, Barry Crowder, Anthony Stallings, and I were trying to make a patriotic statement by recting a flagpole in front of our school. We thought that was news. While the TV station passed on the story, the local newspaper came by dutifully snapped a picture of us shoveling in some concrete. The r story about some grateful kids who wanted to say thanks to their y and the men and women who served it was never told. I learned ng about storytelling and the news business. Seven years later, I produced the 6 P.M. and 10 P.M. newscasts at the same television station that turned us down.

I never told my colleagues at WPSD-TV in Paducah, Kentucky, why I aired so darn many stories about kids doing good things at high schools. It was my own private revenge for getting blown off by the assignment desk when I was seventeen years old. That flag pole story taught me a couple of life-shaping lessons. I learned to listen more carefully when viewers called in with story ideas. And I learned that television journalists have become experts at covering "events" but they needed to tell stories that go beyond the "what" of news.

REMEMBER: Go beyond the simple question of "what" to ask the more complex question of "why." Keep coverage of issues such as crime in proportion to the real threats that your community faces.

DEVELOP AN ONLINE STATE OF MIND

Journalists who do not routinely use the Internet as a reporting tool miss some of the richest listening posts I know. I will not attempt in this chapter to make you an Internet expert, but I do want to raise your awareness to some of the places that I find to be the most useful for reporters who want to go beyond the "what" of stories to find more complexity.

Enterprising journalists fish where the crowd never fishes. I don't spend much time hanging around the most popular Web sites. My favorite sites are:

- *www.Stateline.org.* It indexes top stories from every state at 10 A.M. I look for trends.
- *www.1st Headlines.com.* Constantly updates top news stories.
- *www.washingtonpost.com.* I especially like its education and health sections.
- *www.law.com.* The National Law Review; it tracks lawsuit legal trends.

- *www.philanthropy.org.* The Chronicle of Philanthropy; it is the authority on issues involving charity.

Look in the special projects sections that newspapers and TV stations keep online. The sites usually include work that has been thoroughly researched and fleshed out. Theses are also often the most universal stories.

Some examples of strong stories I have found in online special projects sections include:

- *The Orlando Sentinel's* investigation of mobile home safety and lack of inspection. It included great details about the mobile home industry's political power in Florida. It also pointed out that 100,000 central Florida school children attend classes in mobile homes, to push the story beyond trailer parks.

- *The Austin American-Statesman* produced an impressive investigation of oil pipeline safety in the United States. The paper reported, "Out of sight and unnoticed, America's sprawling oil and natural gas pipelines are leaking on the scale of a ruptured supertanker.

"They are fouling the environment and causing fires and explosions that have killed more than 200 people and injured more than 1,000 in the past decade.

"And the numbers are increasing steadily—from 161 serious incidents in 1989 to 222 in 1999."[7]

The paper pointed out that the pipes lie beneath all of our communities. The paper said, "Thousands of miles of 'gathering lines' are not regulated at all in rural areas, and many of them are known to be leaking. Nationally, there are more than 200,000 miles of these lines, which carry natural gas and crude oil from wellheads to collection points."

- "The Disappearing Songbirds," a magnificent project by *The Atlanta Journal-Constitution.* The story said, "Dozens of Georgia's sweet-sounding songbirds are in serious trouble. Since 1980, more than twenty melodious songsters—including warblers, tanagers and thrushes—have declined at a rate of 1 to 4 percent a year or between eighteen to seventy percent per species."[8] This story is something I just don't expect to see on TV. It is a nice surprise.

When you see remarkable stories online, write a note asking the authors what they *didn't* do but wish they *had* done. Reporters love to

lines: The Invisible Danger," 2 Austin American-Statesman, 22 July 2001, sec. A, p. 1.
Seabrook, "Georgia's Disappearing Songbirds," *The Atlanta Journal-Constitution,* 20
1.

talk about their work and they adore the idea that somebody is interested enough to follow up.

Before you use anything you find online, ask yourself, "What is the source of their information? How do they know what they claim to know? Who stands behind it?" If the story were about a study, poll, or a survey the enterprising journalist should ask, "Why would they sponsor a study like that? What is in it for them? What axes are they grinding" It is fairly easy to find out who owns a Web site and even how to get in touch with the Web site owner. Go to *www.marksonline.com* and enter the Web site name. The name of the registrant will pop up along with a contact phone number.

The saying "You get what you pay for" does not necessarily apply online. There are thousands, maybe millions, of fine Web sites online that are 100 percent free. Sometimes Web versions of stories are more current than print or even broadcast versions. Often Web site stories contain vastly more detail or even the ability to get "micro local" on data. The United States Census (*www.census.gov*) site, for example, has tons of data as specific as individual counties across the United States.

I love listserves. They are a way to gather lots of story ideas without even surfing the Web. There are hundreds of thousands of listservs on every imaginable topic. Lists, sometimes called mail lists, are e-mails that Web sites and organizations send out in huge batches to anyone who signs up for them. Sometimes the list is sent at the same time every day. The lists I find most useful include:

- Gallup weekly update. It alerts you to congressional hearings, upcoming polls, and national pulse numbers. I get at least a story a week from the newsletter. It is free.
- Casey Center for Children newsletter. The weekly newsletter covers issues involving children like nobody else, and the center has a spotless reputation.
- Census weekly update. It sends alerts about new slugs of data coming out, usually with a twenty-four-hour embargo.
- Consumer Product Safety Council. Recalls and safety alerts by e-mail.
- Forbes.com. Daily business briefs by 10 A.M. Monday through Friday.
- Shoptalk. Run by veteran journalist Don Fitzpatrick, Shoptalk is a daily update on television station news, trends, announcements of who got hired or fired.

In addition to listservs, I urge you to discover another online resource—-newsgroups. Newsgroups are discussion groups (that often have nothing to do with news) on every imaginable topic. I once went into a newsgroup to help my sister-in-law buy a new commercial-quality vacuum. No kidding, there was a newsgroup solely dedicated to issues of vacuums. The writers spoke endlessly about what models were best or worst. Some were interested in sweeper history or antiques.

I have used newsgroups to get advice on repairing car paint, unclogging kitchen sinks, and purchasing a digital camera. Journalists sometimes lurk around newsgroups to learn about a particular topic or even to ask for help finding a source or locating a piece of information. The best place to find a newsgroup is Google Groups. Just go to *http://www.google.com* and selecte the "groups" tab. Remember, the messages you post on a newsgroup do not go away. Assume they will be there forever. They are not difficult to search, so assume that anyone could, with a little skill, discover who you are online. Google Groups includes 700 million newsgroup messages spanning twenty years.

Enterprising journalists can also find great stories by reading odd and offbeat publications and Web sites including prison newspapers, college newspapers, high school newspapers. Airliners.net, for example, is a place that tracks hot airline stories and even lists individual pictures of planes in the news by tail number. Business magazines and alt weekly newspapers are also useful. Yahoo does a good job indexing them: *www.dir.yahoo.com/News_and_Media/Newspapers/Alternative_Newsweeklies/*

Enterprising journalists should read lots of newspapers. Especially make it a point to read newspapers from counties outside your metro area. It is nearly effortless to read any newspaper in America.

- Onlinenewspapers.com lists thousands of local newspapers from around the country listed by state and city.

REMEMBER: **Develop an online state of mind to discover information on the Internet that others miss.**

Chapter 11

Surviving and Thriving in Today's TV Newsroom

"If we all do what we can to make the world a better place, the world will be a better place."

MARTIN FLETCHER, NBC NEWS WAR CORRESPONDENT

THIS FINAL CHAPTER MAY SEEM like an odd topic for a book about storytelling and writing. I include these final thoughts because our business is losing too many veteran journalists to burnout, low pay, long hours, separation from family, unskilled management, layoffs, and job stress. One study found that 60 percent of all producers and 53 percent of all reporters surveyed said they had given serious thought to leaving their profession.[1]

In this chapter, I'll explore:

◇ Tips for balancing relationships and work.

◇ Ways to manage your time and stay focused.

◇ Surviving office politics and gossip.

◇ The qualities of a newsroom leader.

◇ How to manage your boss, manage your career, and find meaning for your life.

STRESSED AND OVERWORKED

"This is a 24/7 business and there is no off season," says Patti Dennis, news director at KUSA-TV, Denver.[2] News veterans such as Dennis have

---

[1]"Career Change from TV News," Vernon Stone, professor emeritus, Missouri School of Journalism, surveys 1994–2001.

[2]Patti Dennis, interviewed by the author, October 2000.

learned to create routines in their lives to help offset job stress and balance erratic schedules.

Dennis says she keeps photos of her thirteen- and ten-year-old daughters and her husband in her office to remind her to stay grounded and centered.

"If you want to be in this business long, you want to be in the middle of where things are happening," she says. "That means if you make plans with your family and a big story breaks, your family gets pushed aside. Sometimes you just stay (at the office) because you want to be a part of the coverage." Dennis has spent plenty of nights at the office. She worked two and a half days straight during the Columbine shooting coverage, catching naps on a beanbag chair in the station's Green Room.

In order to spend time with her family, Dennis says her family has had to learn to live their evenings backward. "The kids do baths and homework first. I try to leave work no later than 7 P.M. (a typical day is eleven hours), and we eat dinner at 8:30. My family thinks that is normal. My children will have husbands someday who will ask them, "Why do we eat so late?" Patti calls family dinners "a protected time." "We turn off the TV, we pray and then we talk."

Dennis thinks it is important that news parents realize when they need down time. "You make yourself say it is okay to leave work and have lunch with your kid at school," she says. "I have a pager, a cell phone, and I go sit at school and have lunch. I try to do it once a week."

Clearly, a career in broadcast journalism can be hard on families. Forty-two percent of television newspeople said they had job-related marriage problems, according to research by University of Missouri journalism professor emeritus Dr. Vernon Stone. The numbers were especially high among television executive producers, at 65 percent, and television news directors, at 48 percent.[3]

Stone's study cited that long hours at work were the main reason for the problems at home. Odd and unpredictable work schedules run a close second.[4]

It is difficult to nail down how broadcast journalists' work hours compare with those of the rest of the nation. The rising number of part-time workers, workers with second jobs, and undocumented and unre-

---

"Marriage and TV News," Vernon Stone, professor emeritus, Missouri School of Journalism, ʳeys 1994–2001.

ported workers makes calculating the average workweek an inexact science. But the International Labor Organization estimates the average American works 1,966 hours annually. Harvard University economics professor Juliet Schor, in her book *The Overworked American,* estimated the average full-time worker was putting in a forty-seven-hour workweek.[5] A 1997 study by the National Families and Work Institute calculated the same forty-seven-hour estimate.

Stone's studies say television news journalists work an average of fifty-five hours a week, at least one full eight-hour workday more than the average American's forty-seven hours. Over the course of a year, that's a full month and a half of eight-hour workdays more than the average American.

The stressful environment of newsrooms has become so deeply engrained in newsroom mythology that Hollywood's movies make fun of it. I laugh out loud at films about newsrooms such as *Broadcast News* or *The Paper* because they are exactly the kinds of zoos I have worked in. An hour before newscasts, people begin talking loudly and so quickly that they sound like cartoon characters. These patterns of deadline stress run so deep that we accept stress as an unavoidable part of newsroom culture. Journalists try to relieve stress with a quick drink after work or a workout at the gym. Both are temporary solutions. The workout is a healthier alternative, but even that cannot right a seriously out-of-balance life.

My wife, Sidney, is a marriage and family therapist. She has consulted for dozens of Fortune 500 companies and government agencies that know something about stress, including the Internal Revenue Service. Drawing on her therapist experience and her years being married to a news director, I asked her to come up with some tips for journalists who are trying to balance their personal relationships and their work. She recommends:

- **Your partner is not a mind reader.** You know it has been a busy news day; your partner does not. If you are going to be late for dinner, pick up the phone and call. Your partner most likely understands the nature of the news business, but does not understand why it is so difficult for you to call when you are running late. When you don't call, your partner can only make one assumption: The story that is keeping you at work is more important than your relationship.

[5]Juliet Schor, *The Overworked American* (New York: Basic Books, 1991), 30.

- **Put your mask on first.** Airline flight attendants tell passengers that, in an emergency, the passengers should put their oxygen masks on first before trying to help others. There is a good lesson in this. Journalists must care for themselves and their relationships before they can hope to help their viewers. If your life is out of balance, your stories will reflect that. Worse, others around you will begin to feed off your actions. Newsroom leaders, even informal leaders such as photojournalists, producers, and reporters, set the tone for how others act. Attend school plays, Little League games, and PTA meetings. The most stressed people I know are those who have few interests outside of work. Volunteer to take on assignments for others so they can attend important family events, too. Build a culture in your newsroom for caring about life beyond the newscast.

- **Pictures help.** You live a stress-filled life. Keep pictures in your workspace that remind you of time when you had relaxed fun. Many successful executives I have worked with surround themselves with family pictures that help keep them focused on why they do the important work they do. Usually journalists enter this profession/craft because they want to make the world a better place, not because of the fame or money. Most successful people have an underlying belief that their work is important. It is what keeps them in their job when times get tough and stress throws their life out of whack.

- **Ten minutes and ten seconds.** I often tell couples who walk into my office that their first homework assignment is to spent ten minutes a day talking with each other for one week. When they come to see me a week later, I am not surprised to see that most stressed-out couples can't even complete that one simple assignment. Then, I assign them to spend ten seconds a day kissing. It is surprising how much couples find to talk about after that exercise.

- **The three most important moments.** The three most important moments in a couple's day are when you wake up, when you say goodbye for the day, and when you see each other after the workday is through. How do you say good morning or goodbye? How do you say hello at the end of the workday? Those interactions set the tone for how your partner will think of you all day and how you will interact with each other at the end of the day.

- **Final thoughts:** Your partner and your family share you with the audience. We don't like sitting alone in the bathroom with the kids and the family dog while you cover the tornadoes that are hitting your town. We don't like it when you have to work on Christmas and Thanksgiving. We don't like it when you get called out to cover a big gas leak that keeps you from attending the kid's birthday party or when you miss the funeral of a family friend because it's sweeps month and the office says it can't do without you. They always say that. Be with us as often as you can. Life is short.[6]

It is not just the married journalists who feel the stress of the job in their personal lives. Dr. Stone's survey shows more than half of all TV's single newspeople (52 percent) admit to having job-related difficulties in their personal life. Single journalists say they are unable to get out and meet other singles because of the long and irregular hours. Stone's survey found that, on average, journalists in television move to another city every three years. A TV reporter/weekend anchorwoman, age thirty-one, wrote, "I'm probably not married because I move so much, six jobs and cities in nine years since getting out of school. Each time I had to leave alone."

"My partner and I can't set a wedding date because we can't find jobs in the same city," explained a female TV producer, age twenty-six.

"Someday I'd like to get married and have kids," a female TV reporter, age twenty-four, said. "I've even met a wonderful guy here in town. But I'm so ambitious, I'd leave town to get a better job." Stone says a lot of young singles in the news business will avoid long-term relationships because they know they will be moving in a couple of years.

Many of the survey respondents felt married to their jobs. A female TV reporter, age twenty-six, said, "I often feel I've put my life on hold. Meanwhile, I have virtually no social life."

"I broke up with a live-in girlfriend because she felt my job meant more to me than she did. And it did," a TV anchorman, age twenty-seven, told Stone's survey.[7]

---

[6]Sidney Tompkins, "Keep Your Relationships Healthy," *RTNDA Communicator* (December 2000): 23.

[7]"TV and Radio News jobs keep many unmarried," Dr. Vernon Stone, University of Missouri Department of Journalism, May 25, 2001.

I am convinced that reporters, photojournalists, and producers would be more effective journalists if they could find more balance in their non-news life.

TIME MANAGEMENT

Time is the supreme currency in television. We never seem to have enough time to do all the research we want on stories. There is never enough time to get from one interview to another. There is never enough time to think about the teases that producers write. There is never enough time to hold a truly meaningful morning meeting. We are always in a rush. If only we had time.

From handheld computers to leather-bound organizers, I have tried every time management tool known. Some help me keep track of schedules better than others, but none of these organizers gives me more time. Time management is a team sport. Reporters, producers, and photojournalists know that, in a newsroom, others often manage your time for you. Photojournalists know that when a reporter drones on endlessly in an interview or delays writing the story until the last minute, the story editing will be a last-minute rush job no matter how well the photojournalist has done his job. Producers who manage their day with maximum efficiency can't overcome reporters who file stories at the last minute. Reporters who work efficiently have no control over producers who change the show rundown at the last minute and now want a live shot, which will require the reporter to dash out the door and meet the live truck.

Newsrooms that value time management must value goal setting. They also must respect how individual decisions affect others. As a manager I became interested in how much time I wasted every day just waiting for others to show up to meetings. It was not uncommon for me to have six or seven meetings of various sorts a day. If I waited five minutes to start each one, and five minutes was the minimum I usually had to wait, that was thirty-five minutes a day that I was wasting. That was equal to more than a full workday a month, more than one full workweek a year that I was idling away waiting for meetings to start. I grew to have little patience for people who would show up to meetings late and unprepared. When you get to meetings, explain your ideas clearly and efficiently. Don't argue just to make noise, but don't go along just to save time. Respect the fact that other people have time pressures and do all you can to recognize what affect your decision has on their lives.

One of the Ten Commandments is "thou shalt not steal." Keep it by not stealing others' time.

At Thanksgiving, 2001, a producer friend of mine was telling me how frustrated she was that reporters were balking at doing live shots. They wanted to finish their stories and go home. I asked my friend how important the live shots were to the *viewer*, not just to the producers. I asked whether the reporter might use the time that would be spent driving to the live shot in some more productive way, such as setting up a story for the next day or making sure all of the supers were correctly typed. I asked if the good will that might result from allowing the reporter and photo-journalist to duck out of the office a half-hour early on a holiday might build good will that the producer could cash in some other day.

AVOID OFFICE GOSSIP AND POLITICS

Journalists are professional skeptics, gossips, busybodies, politicians, and complainers. We snoop into other people's business for a living. The very qualities that make journalists good at what they do often make us difficult to work with.

The story goes that someone once asked one of the world's most renowned mathematicians to pass along his formula for success in the workplace. He came up with a formula.

$$A = \text{success at work}$$

So the way to achieve it is:

$$A = X + Y + Z$$

In this case, he said, X is represented by doing meaningful work and Y is appropriate compensation for the work done.

"What is Z?" someone asked.

"Z is knowing when to keep your mouth shut around colleagues," he said.

I have found that the least productive people in my newsroom were the worst gossips. I am not sure if they were unproductive because they spent their time gossiping or if they gossiped because they themselves were so unproductive. Self-confident people have no need to harm others with idle rumors. I have to admit that when I was a reporter, I spent too much time mining newsroom sources to learn who was moving up, down, or out the door. Those of us who worked in the special projects and investigations unit lived in daily fear that our unit was going to be dissolved. Even when our news director would assure us we were not going to be fired, we wondered why he took time to say that. Certainly that meant that somebody was considering it or he would not mention it for a denial.

When I became a news director, I learned that most office gossip was born when there was not enough real information available to people. The rumors would fly highest when I could not reveal information about an employee's firing, personal troubles, or disciplinary action. The best rumor control in any newsroom is an open pipeline of information from the managers to the newsroom and from the newsroom to the managers. When somebody comes to you with gossip about another person, let him or her know you are not interested.

LEADERS IN THE NEWSROOM

Some journalists work a full, productive career in newsrooms and do not alienate their co-workers in the process. What habits have they formed to stay focused on the important work they have to do? I consulted three respected reporters: Nancy Amons (WSMV-TV, Nashville), Chuck Goudie (WLS-TV, Chicago), and Bill Sheil (WJW-TV, Cleveland). Together, we developed a blueprint for journalists who want to become newsroom leaders—the kind of people who do not just survive but thrive, even in tough times.

• **Become the "go-to" person in daily news and breaking news events, even if you work a specific beat or produce a specific show.** Reporters, producers, and photojournalists become indispensable when they become the "go to" person in their newsroom for daily events, not just special sweeps or promotions projects. Even on daily deadline stories, look for the story that others, who do not have your enterprising eye, will never find. Pitch in without being asked. Go for the "big get" that others might give up on after day one. When the big story hits, be the producer who volunteers to pull together special coverage. Be the reporter who has prepared for this day by keeping emergency contact information ready at your fingertips. Be the photojounalist who already has charged his camera batteries, packed his gear, and filled his news car with gas. These people have a "put me in the game" attitude. They have a bias toward action.

• **Be on the truth squad.** Allow others to learn from their mistakes, but do not allow the kinds of mistakes on the air that will cause real harm. Think of this the way a flight instructor thinks of it. A student pilot makes mistakes, but the instructor cannot allow the plane to crash and burn. So the instructor waits until the critical point that the student realizes the mistake but the plane can still be controlled. *Flight instructors never permit the sort of mistake that can be made only once.*

Journalists can follow that guide. I can remember, as a reporter, seeing information in other people's lead-ins or teases that I knew or believed was not true. Yet I wanted to be careful about the delicate position of questioning somebody else's story or the contents of another producer's newscast. My Poynter colleague Jill Geisler says journalists must learn the difference between "rescuing" and "redecorating." You rescue stories that will be wrong and cause harm if they air as is. You redecorate when you substitute your words for the writer's words, editing mostly for style and not for truth and substance. Writers hate that kind of editing. It steals credit for the work and it undermines the writer's confidence.

So don't become the newsroom's "Bigfoot," but do not be timid or quiet when your newsroom is about to broadcast information you can help prove is incorrect or out of context. Ask, "How do we know that?" "What assumptions did our source make that we will pass along to the viewers as fact?" To build the kind of culture that would invite such input, be sure that you are open for others to ask questions about your work that could make it stronger. Whenever possible, ask challenging questions in private, not in front of the boss or colleagues. Remember the old saying, "Criticism should arrive in private but delivering praise should be a public event."

• **Be a teacher, mentor, and coach.** Be willing to teach others how to use enterprise and investigative tools such as Internet sites, public record databases, and other resources. Be selfless. Be willing to turn information over to others and resist the temptation to do everything yourself.

- Coaches teach people, while fixers focus just on the story or the copy.

- Coaches work front-end before problems develop. Fixers work on deadline at the last minute.
- Coaches deflect credit, but fixers steal credit by "saving the day" at the last minute.
- Coaches focus on what works in a story, but fixers only focus on what is broken.
- Coaches teach by asking questions to help others strengthen their story or idea, but fixers make firm statements about what is wrong with a story.
- Coaches find themselves being needed less and less, but fixers must fix the same problems over and over.

• **Under-promise, over-deliver.** Even when I thought I had a very good story, I would usually tell my boss I thought the story would be "pretty good." I have worked with plenty of reporters who, every day, would promise the greatest story ever told on television, only to produce garden-variety pieces. I am not suggesting you undersell your story so much that producers do not know where to properly play it. But I would avoid hype and self-promotion. When you say you have the goods, producers and promotions directors want to book it. Don't promise a blockbuster story unless you can over-deliver it. Success has many authors; failure is an orphan.

• **Be the champion of your own promotion.** Reporters and producers should advocate stories to the marketing and promotion department. Take ownership of the need for the promotions to be fair and accurate. Remember that you have a duty not only to your station/network but also to the people involved in and affected by the stories. An awful lot of legal problems that TV newsrooms encounter have little to do with the stories they air. The stories sometimes go though not one lawyer, but two or more, in what ABC News *20/20* senior producer Roberta Baskin once described to me as a "double-lawyerectomy." But the promotions and headlines and teases often do not undergo such scrutiny. It is especially true for daily news stories. Take responsibility for everything that is said on the air about your story.

• **Take ownership of management decisions and find ways to be openly supportive.** This is not to be a management "suck-up." Be a part of a team in which your future and the future of the entire team are invested. Make the group decisions as good as they can be and support them without violating your principles. Even when you disagree with a decision, focus on the decision or policy you want to change, not the individual who made the policy. Take a lesson from politicians on this point. You don't hear politicians say, "My colleague is an idiot and a liar." They say, "My esteemed colleague has more experience than I do in this area, but we don't always agree, and this is one of those areas where we need to find more common ground." Disagreements in newsrooms are fine; in fact, we should encourage the robust contrarian voice in our newsroom. But personal attacks have no place in any news organization.

• **Be an adviser to your boss.** Be strong enough to give him or her the bad news. Help your boss know what is really happening out in the trenches. John Lansing, the senior vice president for broadcast at Scripps Howard told his general managers, "I appreciate bad news, because it means you are being honest with me."[8] John, of course, wants to hear honestly stated good news, too.

Don't communicate with your boss *only* when you need something. Help him or her know when some little thing is going well in the newsroom. Deliver some good news to your boss once in a while. Even better, deliver some good news that is not about something *you* did. Tell your boss about a co-worker who made an extra effort or showed uncommon caring to resolve a viewer's complaint. Dub off a story that somebody else did but the news director might have missed.

When I was a news director I became aware that not much good news comes walking through the office door each day. The most common sound any news director hears is "Knock-knock; got a minute?" I knew full well that not one person who asked for a minute of my time only wanted a minute. The never-ending parade at my door included:

"Knock-knock; got a minute? I think you should know, I am getting a divorce."

"Knock-knock; got a minute? I think I am going to quit."

"Knock-knock; got a minute? I am having problems with my kid. I need to be off early every Wednesday so we can go to counseling."

"Knock-knock; got a minute? The TV media critic called me and asked about rumors that our weekend anchors are fighting. Should I have spoken with him?"

"Knock-knock; got a minute? Don't be surprised if the chief of (fill in the name of a city/town/village or state police department) calls to complain about me. I just want you to know he is a jerk and don't believe anything he says."

---

[8]John Lansing, interviewed by the author, December 4, 2001, Tampa, Florida.

"Knock-knock; got a minute? My (grandmother, grandfather, cat, car) died. I won't be in tomorrow."

"Knock-knock; got a minute? Corporate needs you to submit a plan to cut spending by $100,000. They need it in 48 hours."

"Knock-knock; got a minute? One of the photographers wrecked a station car. It's the second time this year. Did you know he has a drinking problem?"

"Knock-knock; got a minute? I don't think I will be able to turn that project for sweeps. Will that be a problem?"

Before I sat in that office myself, it never occurred to me that a news director would hear so many stories of sorrow and woe that had next to nothing to do with the *stories* we were putting on TV that night. Yet, these issues were far more important because they had to do with the *people* who were putting the stories on TV.

Know your boss' schedule. If he or she is busy with a big request from corporate, it may not be the best time to drop by and "chew the fat." If your boss is under pressure to cut expenses, it is not the best time to go in to ask for a raise. I also learned to ask the boss' secretary who had been in the office before I stepped in there. If a "problem child" had just been warming the chair, I might reschedule to a time when I could get a better warmer reception.

• **Manage the boss.** I often hear reporters and producers claim that their boss does not know them. They say the boss only thinks of them as employees, not as real people. Bosses feel the same way. If you really want to be effective, get to know your boss' style. I worked for two general managers in my career as news director. The first of them, Mike Kettenring, loved for me to generate detailed reports. The more paper, it seemed, the better. Mike, a deeply principled man, was schooled by the Jesuits. He rose to station management having been a news director. He wore stiffly starched shirts and was so organized that he wanted his reports delivered with three holes pre-punched and ready to be inserted into chronologically arranged binders behind his spotless desk. If I told Mike he could expect a project to be completed by June 14, then I would get a note from him on June 7 saying, "Status? Respond by June 10." Mike believed in an ordered life. He became a Catholic priest. No person, with the exceptions of my mother and my wife, influenced my life more.

My next general manager, Frank DeTillio, is a master salesman. Once a person tells Frank his or her name, Frank never has to ask again.

He takes pride in remembering people's names. By the second meeting, he makes it his business to discover something unique about the individual; where the person grew up, went to school, what that person's father did for a living. He is a marvelously warm, fun-loving, and caring man who became frustrated with my non-stop snowstorm of written reports to him. I had grown into that habit with Mike and assumed all general managers wanted a daily dose of paperwork from me. I couldn't understand his need to see me face-to-face every day. Frank taught me the value of learning the needs and desires of the customers and viewers and, so long as it didn't violate our company principles, to adapt to that style.

The main lesson I learned from these two different styles is "learn how your boss wants to be communicated with." Do they like information in a written report, e-mail, voice-mail, or face to face? Do they want you to go through a formal chain of command or do they appreciate a less formal and direct style? Do they like people to drop by the office or do they want you to make an appointment? Are they detail-oriented people, like my first GM was or do they want executive summaries, like my second GM preferred? Does your boss want to be called at home when a story breaks, or does he or she want you to handle it and only call in an extreme emergency? Managing the boss is not the same as "sucking up to the boss." Managing the boss means seeing the whole person, just as you want the boss to see you.

• **Have your facts straight.** There is nothing more frustrating for a news director as when a producer, for example, marches in and says that the graphics department has gotten an over-the-shoulder graphic wrong for the third straight week. So the news director marches in to the head of the graphics area and begins to vent about the need for accuracy and accountability. The graphics folks tell the news director that the producer has a habit of coming in at the last minute with her requests and she rarely fills out a written graphics order. The artists say they are trying to understand what the producer wants while they are working on a half-dozen other requests—and that is how the mistakes happen. But the producer has complained she does not have time for their silly written requests. The news director now has to remove his foot from his mouth and the egg from his face. He will have a difficult time believing the producer again. He might also wonder if the producer is that careless in leaving out essential facts in her newscasts.

I deeply appreciated those who would come in to a short meeting with a list of things they needed action on. They would offer options. They would have done their homework.

Reporter Nancy Amons once came to me with a request to buy a fast new computer that she said she needed to do some complex database work in her investigative reporting. She didn't just "drop by" the office. She made an appointment, got there on time and she didn't waste time with chitchat; she came right to the point. She said she knew money was tight. She said she understood the difference between "want" and "need" and she wanted to convince me that this was a "need." She handed me color brochures of the machine. She had a copy for herself so she could answer questions as we went along. She had researched the costs, including shipping costs and tax. She knew what the associated software would cost and she volunteered to teach herself how to use the spreadsheet programs she would have to know to use the machine. She gave me a couple of less expensive options but explained why they were not great choices for what she planned to do. She said there was no need for a new monitor, the old one would work fine. She just wanted the computer. When I said yes, and she got the machine, Nancy sent me a note of thanks and within a short time after the new computer's arrival she produced a story that we could not have produced without the database work.

I remember how she came into the office and told me that because of my good decision to buy the computer *we* had produced an important story. We both knew the truth; it was her reporting and vision and not mine that produced the work, but it made me more eager to purchase other equipment and software. Nancy Amons always managed *me* more than I managed *her*.

• **Value the judgments and contributions of others.** The best journalists I know are not only highly skilled and experienced; they also listen to and respect the ideas of others, including directors, graphic artists, and photojournalists. Colleagues who are not involved in minute-to-minute coverage may see stories quite differently from journalists who get caught up in the daily news grind. Allow others to help you discover that there is not one truth but many truths.

• **Discover all you can about your viewers, and seek to serve them.** Draw from personal experience, research, and a wide network of diverse contacts. Viewers are usually not at all like journalists in the way they live, think, or view the content and execution of newscasts. I sometimes ask my workshop participants to hold their hand up if they have a hunting license, even in rural areas of this country. Almost no hands go up. I ask how many go fishing once a month or more. A few more hands go up. I ask how many drive a pickup truck. A few more hands go up. I ask them how many hands I would see if I asked their viewers those questions. They often laugh and say they see my point. Journalists are not at all like many of their viewers. Our communities are far more diverse than most of our newsrooms.

• **Be a writing and ethics example.** Uphold high standards for storytelling and news gathering. Find ways to recognize the good work of others even if you are not their boss. By affirming the work of others, you are sharing and multiplying your own values. In every newsroom I have worked in, the most powerful leaders were not the people in formal authority, but were the most respected journalists who taught and supported others. Managers should not be the only ones in the newsroom who are willing to make tough ethics calls. Manage up your ethics.

• **Anticipate major events.** Be an example of front-end thinking. Help others to think ahead about what graphics, technical capabilities, personnel, and information you will need to cover a big planned story. You know that there will be elections, holidays, Olympics, inaugurations, trials, hearings, and legislative sessions. Even if those whose formal job it is to plan for such events do not think as forwardly as you would like, take responsibility to do so yourself.

• **Know your industry.** Read Poynter.org, *Shoptalk, Electronic Media, Broadcasting & Cable.* Get plugged in to what is happening in our industry. The most successful journalists I know have wide networks of contacts at other stations in other cities. They often discuss story ideas with others and adapt good ideas from other places to their own reporting. Understand how ratings work. It is naïve to think that a journalist's job is just to report the news. Journalists should understand their own business in order to argue in favor of strong coverage. I have known so many reporters who get stuck doing silly stories because some manager said research indicated that story is what the viewers want to see.

I tell reporters to ask more questions. Ask if they can see the research, not as a challenge to the story idea, but to understand what the viewers seem to be saying. Even if management is unwilling to share the research documents, maybe they would be willing to conduct a newsroom meeting to explain the results and how that affects storytelling and story selection.

The number of reporters and producers and photojournalists who admit to me that they don't understand how the ratings system works surprises me. Here are a few things every broadcast journalists should know about ratings:

Nielsen Media Research has become the de facto national measurement for the television industry in the United States and Canada. Nielsen uses a technique called statistical sampling to rate shows, which is essentially the same technique that pollsters use to predict outcomes. For that reason, I urge all journalists to remember that ratings are "estimates" not "facts." They are NOT accurate to a tenth of a point, as so many stations pretend them to be when they are claiming a rating victory.

Nationwide, Nielsen measures about 5,000 households of the ninety-nine million American households by installing with TV meters.[9] The meters are little black boxes, which include a computer and a modem that monitor what the household has watched that day. Every night the modem dials Nielsen and downloads the information. Of course, the meter has no way of knowing how many people watched TV or even if anybody was in the room. To try to check the accuracy of the meters, the company also mails out diaries. Diaries are filled out in quarter-hour increments, while meters capture viewing in seconds. Meters pick up channel surfing but diaries don't. Diaries are prone to socially based responses such as "I watch PBS all the time," while meters are more likely to show that people really watch *America's Scariest Home Videos.* Younger viewers are less diligent than older viewers in filling out diaries. According to NBC vice president for entertainment Deborah Hamberlin, "Younger skewing programs and stations are underreported in diaries but almost always do better when they are metered." Diaries have a short life span; each week diaries are sent to different households in the market. The meter sample stays in place for up to five years.[10]

How to score: For your station to get credit for a quarter-hour, a meter must record that a TV set was tuned to your station for five minutes. The five minutes do not have to be consecutive, and it is possible for more than one station to get credit for a single quarter hour.

The lead-in: If you look in all of the metered markets, you will find very few stations that lose the lead-in program and win the news pro-

---

[9]"How Does Nielsen Media Research Know Who Is Watching?", *http://www.nielsenmedia.com/wtrrm.html.*

[10]Deborah Hamberlin, "Must Read TV," *NBC Promotions Newsletter* (Winter 1997): 6.

gram, especially in early evenings. You must promote the programs that play just before your early and late news and promote the news itself.

Ratings and shares: In most markets only 400 households are metered and fewer are actually counted (in tab) on any given day because of cable outages, power interruptions, or other issues. This means that three or four households could determine one household ratings point. A rating point is the size of an audience expressed as a percentage of the total target audience universe. Share means the percentage of all televisions in use that are tuned to a specific station or program. Most stations have someone, usually in the sales department, who specializes in analyzing ratings trends. Take them to lunch and get a lesson in ratings and audience flow.

In addition to understanding how the ratings system works, I offer what, to some, might be a controversial suggestion: Journalists should learn more about who pays their bills. Plenty of right-minded journalists disagree with me on this point. They say that a reporter's only concern should be telling the news. I may have thought that when I was a reporter. But when I became a news director I had a new appreciation for reporters who knew when they were about to step on the toes of a major advertiser. I appreciated the awareness, not because we were going to avoid stepping on those toes, but so we could forewarn the sales and station management that there was going to be trouble on the phone soon. Remember that as a producer or a reporter, you are only one of several stakeholders at the station. Other people, including account executives and other managers, will be affected by your reporting. Be an aggressive and fair journalist *and* respect others.

• **Remember that hard-hitting stories and newscasts sometimes have ripple effects.** Sales and management are not the only ones who will be affected by your stories. Other reporters may have a harder time getting information from the police after you rip the Police Department for a problem you discovered. Lawsuits that get filed over your stories, even if they are groundless, touch many lives beyond your own. Colleagues may be called to testify about a story, the station may have to spend thousands or even millions of dollars defending your reporting. Be bold and aggressive, but be sensitive to the ripple effect of your stories. Be open and even invite conversation from colleagues about the challenges your stories create for others.

• **Come to work with "first-day enthusiasm."** I wish that reporters and photojournalists could find a way to stay in their professions longer.

I wish that more journalists would establish deep roots in a community rather than shallow roots in many communities as they move from market to market with the regularity of college football coaches. When reporters constantly move from market to market, the viewers lose. The viewers often know more about their town's history and values than the journalists do.

THE MEANING OF LIFE

"I figured out what life is all about," Ron Tindiglia told one of his friends while on a fishing trip. After nearly thirty years as a broadcast news management icon in New York and Los Angeles, Ron was dying of cancer.

It was such a typical soundbite from this man who touched so many. For three years before his death, I was privileged to learn so much from this master of news management. He often called to ask what I was doing. I would tell him about all of the big plans I had for our newsroom, about good things we had done, and he was like an adoring father. He rarely told me about his own achievements; he just asked about mine. I considered him one of my most trusted "rabbis." At his funeral, I realized that there must have been 200 people who thought they had the same relationship with him. There, at his funeral, Ron had one more thing to teach us.

We learned it from friends who delivered his eulogy. They used Ron's words to tell a story, from which, we would all learn the meaning of life.

"See, life has stages," Ron said. The first stage is the stage where all you want to do is get "stuff." In order to get stuff, you work to get money. In this phase you work to make a living. The work is a means to an end.

The second stage, Ron said, is about getting "better stuff." Just having stuff is not good enough anymore. Now we need bigger, better more expensive stuff. The clothes, the cars, the house, the good stuff. Instead of buying used cars, you buy a new one. You work so hard that you need a motorcycle or a big stereo to medicate your stress and unhappiness. You deserve the luxury; you work hard for it.

Then, if you are lucky, you get discontent with the second stage and you pass into the third phase of life. The third phase has to do with the search for life's meaning. It is no longer about stuff. In fact it is the "anti-stuff" phase. Work takes on a new urgency, a new depth, and a new importance. The third phase is about leaving a legacy. It is about living out what you have spent your life claiming that you stand for.

The old country wisdom I grew up with applies—"Saying *ain't* doing." Journalists must actively nurture, value, and defend the individual's right to express ideas even if they are unpopular. Do all you can to keep government records as open as possible and to keep the press as free as possible to report the truth, however you find it. Our democracy depends on the free flow of information to the people. Consider the fact that there has never been a famine in a country that has a free and aggressive press. Journalists like you would find out why the food is not getting to where it is needed most and you would hold the system responsible. The Constitution of the United States only mentions one profession, journalism, for specific protection.

Respect the viewers, speak to their hearts and minds. Don't waste their time.

Tell the truth as fully and courageously as possible.

Seek many voices.

Practice ethics.

Enterprise more.

Question everything.

Reject conventional wisdom.

Strive for excellence.

Take better care of yourself.

Use active verbs.

And aim for the heart.

INDEX